The
Lone Star State
Divided
Texans and the Civil War

The
Lone Star State
Divided

Texans and the Civil War

Merle Durham

Hendrick-Long Publishing Co.
DALLAS

Illustrations courtesy of
Chapter 1: Page 5, #38219 Collection of The New-York Historical Society, New York, New York; 6, Library of Congress; 7, The Center for American History, The University of Texas at Austin; **Chapter 2:** 8, Hendrick-Long Collection; 10, The Center for American History, The University of Texas at Austin; 12, #50733 Collection of The New-York Historical Society, New York, New York; **Chapter 3:** 14, #ICHi-11657 Chicago Historical Society; 15, Amon Carter Museum, Fort Worth; 16, The Center for American History, The University of Texas at Austin; **Chapter 4:** 21, 23, The Center for American History, The University of Texas at Austin; 22, Hendrick-Long Collection; **Chapter 5:** 24, 26, The Center for American History, The University of Texas at Austin; **Chapter 6:** 29, Hendrick-Long Collection; 32, The Witte Museum and the San Antonio Museum Association, San Antonio, Texas; 33, 35, The Center for American History, The University of Texas at Austin; 37, Ellen S. Brockenbrough Library, The Museum of the Confederacy, Richmond, Virginia; **Chapter 7:** 42, Western History Collections, University of Oklahoma Library; **Chapter 8:** 52, The Rosenberg Library, Galveston, Texas; 54, Civil War Photograph Album, Louisiana and Lower Mississippi Valley Collections, LSU Libraries, Louisiana State University; 55, Texas State Library; **Chapter 9:** 58, Hendrick-Long Collection; **Chapter 10:** 63, Institute of Texan Cultures, San Antonio, Texas; **Chapter 11:** 68, Hendrick-Long Collection; **Chapter 13;** 79, Hendrick-Long Collection; **Chapter 14:** 84, Special Collections Division, The University of Texas at Arlington Libraries, Arlington, Texas; **Chapter 16:** 90, 91, 92, Library of Congress; **Chapter 18:** 98, The General Libraries of The University of Texas at Austin, Benson Latin American Collection; 101, Hendrick-Long Collection; **Chapter 19:** 108, Hendrick-Long Collection; 110, Library of Congress; 111, 113, 114, The Center for American History, The University of Texas at Austin; **Chapter 20:** 116, 119, Hendrick-Long Collection

Library of Congress Cataloging-in-Publication Data

Durham, Merle.
    The Lone Star State divided: Texans and the Civil War/by
    Merle Durham.
      p. cm.
    Includes bibliographical references (p.) and index.
    ISBN 0-937460-97-4
    1. Texas—History—Civil War, 1861–1865—Juvenile literature.
    [1. Texas—History—Civil War, 1861–1865.]
    E532.D87 1994   94–1984
    973.7'3'09764—dc20   CIP
                                  AC

Design and Production:
Dodson Publication Services, Austin, Texas

Hendrick-Long Publishing Co.
Dallas, Texas 75225

Table of Contents

Foreword

From the time Fort Sumter was seized on April 12, 1861, until Magruder and Kirby Smith surrendered on June 2, 1865, this war became the most costly in human life, property, and government expenditure ever fought by Americans. Among the leaders who anticipated war, Confederate Secretary of State Robert Toombs warned before the attack on Fort Sumter, "The firing upon that fort will inaugurate a civil war greater than any the world has yet seen." True to his prediction, over 600,000 soldiers died, a greater combined total than the 116,500 Americans who died in World War I and the 405,400 in World War II.

Even though the main theater of the Civil War was east of the Mississippi River, important battles took place in Texas. The Lone Star State furnished a greater percentage of troops than any other state. More than 60,000 Texans, many of whom were under 21 years of age, fought east and west of the Mississippi River. One-fourth of them were killed or lamed.

At the start of the war, many leaders felt it would not last long. Lincoln expected it to be of such short duration that he put out a call for only 75,000 troops for 90 days. President Davis, harboring the same thoughts, called volunteers for 12 months even though some of his officers expected the conflict to last only two months. Time proved them to be wrong. The war stretched on through four unbelievably destructive years. Numbers of armed forces reached into the hundred thousands, with forces of the North greatly outnumbering those of the South. Soldiers of both the North and South served bravely, and those on each side believed their cause was right.

1

Secession

When the war started in 1861, the North was already established in manufacturing, while the Southern economy centered on agriculture. Different needs for the two ways of life caused discord. There were disagreements over high tariffs that benefited only the North. There were conflicts over distribution of public lands and rights of individual states. There was constant criticism against the South's use of slaves, a practice not used in the North. Crusades were organized to abolish

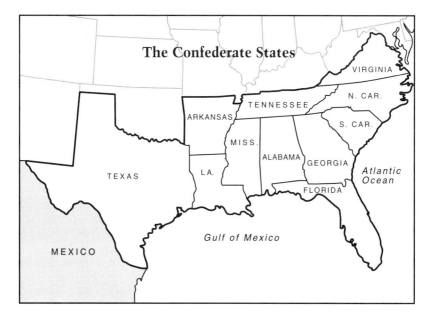

The Confederate States

John Brown became a hero to the anti-slavery crusade.

slavery, and literature was written to encourage rebellion among the slaves.

One of the most famous crusaders against slavery was John Brown, who spent his life shifting from place to place and failing in many different jobs. He worked in Ohio. He moved to Pennsylvania, then to Massachusetts, and later to New York. During his moves, he helped slaves escape to Canada many times. Before Kansas leaders reached a decision on whether to be a free or a slave state, John Brown and his family moved to Kansas and caused serious trouble. In one raid, he and some of his helpers murdered five men who were slave owners. Later, on October 16, 1859, he and 18 followers, including three of his sons, captured the arsenal and army at Harpers Ferry, Virginia, and seized weapons to be used in slave uprisings. Two days later, Robert E. Lee was sent with a company of marines to arrest him. When Brown was brought to trial, he was charged with treason against the state of Virginia, inciting slave rebellion, and murder. He and six of his men were hanged on December 2. The trouble at Harpers Ferry brought fear to people of the South—the fear that others would be influenced to start slave uprisings.

Literature published by anti-slavery writers stirred more trouble between the South and the North. Over 20 years before the war, a pamphlet, *Slavery As It Is, the Testimony of a Thousand Witnesses*, was written by Theodore Dwight Weld of the American Anti-Slavery Society. Among people influenced by this paper was Harriet Beecher Stowe. She used information from Weld's work to write her book *Uncle Tom's Cabin*, which told of the brutality against slaves. She thought her story, published in both English and German, would cause all slave owners to set slaves free. It became a best seller. Ranging in price from 37 1/2 cents each to $1.50 each, 100,000 copies of the book were sold within two months of its publication in 1852. Three hundred thousand more copies were sold within a year.

135,000 SETS, 270,000 VOLUMES SOLD.

UNCLE TOM'S CABIN

FOR SALE HERE.

AN EDITION FOR THE MILLION, COMPLETE IN 1 Vol, PRICE 37 1-2 CENTS.
" " IN GERMAN, IN 1 Vol, PRICE 50 CENTS.
" " IN 2 Vols, CLOTH, 6 PLATES, PRICE $1.50.
SUPERB ILLUSTRATED EDITION, IN 1 Vol, WITH 153 ENGRAVINGS,
PRICES FROM $2.50 TO $5.00.

The Greatest Book of the Age.

Advertisement for Uncle Tom's Cabin

A problem that had brewed for many years reached its peak when Abraham Lincoln was elected president of the United States. Throughout his career as a lawyer and as a member of Congress, the new president had voiced strong objections to slavery. Suspecting he would restrict the practice or even abolish it, many leaders of the South turned their thoughts to secession.

The idea of secession, or breaking away from the country, was not new. From time to time since the beginning of the United States, various states had threatened to secede. Many Americans had always held the idea that a state had the right to withdraw any time it chose to do so. New England states, with an economy based on shipbuilding and commerce, had seriously considered leaving the Union a few years before the War of 1812. These states had become wealthy trading with France and Great Britain, but trouble between the two European countries caused the United States to pass the Embargo Act, which closed ports to all foreign trade.

Abraham Lincoln was unpopular in Texas because of his anti-slavery views.

Overseas trading almost stopped, forcing many ship-builders to close their busi-nesses. Later, secession was considered two more times. First, when New England states objected to the annexa-tion of Texas and the war with Mexico, and second, when South Carolina leaders tried to get rid of a tariff law that they considered to be unfair.

Just six weeks after Lin-coln's election, South Carolina seceded from the United States. Then, only a month later, in January, 1861, five more of the fifteen slave states followed: Mississippi, Florida, Alabama, Georgia, and Louis-iana. On February 4, leaders of the six states met in Mont-gomery, Alabama, to set up a temporary government named The Confederate States of America. They elected Jefferson Davis president and Alexander H. Stephens vice president.

When Davis received word that he had been elected, he and his wife were working in their rose garden at Brierfield, their Mississippi home and plantation. Mrs. Davis noticed a disturbed look on her husband's face as he read the message. Being a strong believer in his coun-try, Davis had spent most of his adult life serving the United States. He was born in Kentucky but moved to Mississippi with his family while he was a child. After graduating from Transylvania University and West Point, he fought on the Wisconsin frontier and in campaigns against Indians, then he served in Congress until the start of the Mexican War. During the war, he was cited for bravery and for his ingenious deployment of troops that won the battle of Buena Vista. During that battle, he fought an entire day with a bullet in his foot. In 1853, while serving as secretary of war, Davis improved and enlarged the army, introduced a new system of infantry tactics, and brought in better weapons. He also organized companies of engineers to explore routes for building railroads from the Mississippi River westward to the Pacific coast.

Jefferson Davis was elected president of the Confederate States.

With such a background, it is no wonder Davis was disturbed. He was not in favor of breaking away from his country, but after his state seceded, he had no choice. Even though he had hoped to be assigned to military duty, he consented to serve as president. After saying goodbye to his slaves and taking a long look at his beautiful home at Brierfield, he boarded a train and left for Montgomery. On the way, the train stopped in many towns. The new president addressed large crowds from the rear platform of the train. He told them that trying times were ahead, and that he hoped the separation from the Union, which was finally inevitable, would be made in peace. There were rousing cheers as Davis spoke. Bands played. One Northern newspaper warned that the new Confederate president was being welcomed by enthusiastic Southern crowds who showed determination to stand by Davis and the new government.

2

Texas Leaves the Union

While the first six states were seceding, Texans were in turmoil. Should they leave the Union? Would slavery be abolished after Lincoln was elected? Even though 95 percent of all Texans did not own slaves, the state's economic system was hinged on large plantation crops grown by slaves. Without slaves, what would happen to the state's economy? Texans had worried over this same problem before.

The state's economic system hinged on the plantation crops grown by the slaves.

There was almost constant fear of slave uprisings. From time to time, there were reports that Texas slaves were hiding arms and gunpowder. Then, some Northern crusades began directing themselves specifically against Texas. Preacher and writer Edward Everett Hale, famous author of *Man Without a Country*, wrote a paper, *How to Conquer Texas Before Texas Conquers Us*. Another crusader drew up a plan to declare war against the Lone Star State and to take it over by military force. Most plots, though, centered on flooding the state with people from the North who would grow cotton without using slaves. This idea became widespread after *Journey Through Texas* was published in 1857. The book was written by Fred Olmsted, who had traveled through the state in the early 1850s observing German settlers who grew vast acres of cotton without using slaves. Olmsted outlined a plan demonstrating how all Texans could grow the valuable crop in the same way.

The secret society Knights of the Golden Circle, formed several years before the start of the war, caused more trouble. Its mission was to expand slavery in order to control the cotton, sugar, tobacco, and rice markets. The year the war started, the society reached its peak and made two attempts to take over Mexico. Even though its efforts failed, the secret group brought more unrest in Texas.

Sam Houston, who had fought and worked for Texas for many years, was very much against secession. After Lincoln was elected, the old warrior refused to side with leaders who declared that the new president's election was equivalent to a declaration of war. Houston felt the South would be much better off as a part of the Union than separated from it. When other Texas leaders called for a special session of Congress to organize a secession convention, Houston refused to allow it. Despite his opposition, Congressional members met and voted to

Sam Houston was against secession.

hold the convention in Austin on January 28, 1861.

When the convention assembled, Oran M. Roberts, associate judge of the Texas Supreme Court, was elected to preside as president. An ordinance of secession was quickly adopted by a vote of 166 to 8. The instrument stated that since the government of the United States was using its power to destroy the prosperity of Texas, it was now returning to its independent republic standing. On February 23, 1861, a public vote was taken in which a majority of Texas citizens approved secession. In the meantime, five days before, on February 18, seven Texas delegates had arrived in Montgomery, Alabama, and were attending the convention forming the new country, The Confederate States of America. In the Texas convention's final assembly, delegates approved the Confederacy's constitution and the new 1861 Constitution of Texas.

In order to remain governor of Texas, Houston was required to take an oath of allegiance to The Confederate States of America. When he refused, his office was declared vacant, and Lieutenant Governor Edward Clark took his place. Eber W. Cave, a well-known newspaper owner and editor who was now serving as secretary of state, was also removed from office when he refused to pledge allegiance to the Confederacy.

When President Lincoln learned what was happening, he sent a message to Houston offering 50,000 troops and all needed military supplies to use force to keep Texas in the Union. Houston felt that Texas had been through enough war—fighting Indians, for independence, and in the war with Mexico. He stood before several Union friends while burning the message and stated, "I love Texas too well to bring strife and bloodshed upon her."

Traveling in a buggy, Houston went from town to town and from plantation to plantation pleading with Texans not to leave the Union. Over and over he warned that secession would bring war, and that war would bring defeat. Despite all his efforts, he finally realized that a majority of Texans were in favor of secession. The old warrior made a final effort to keep Texas in the United States by writing an address to all Texans. "I protest in the name of the People of Texas against all the acts and doings of the convention, and declare them null and void." When his plea was ignored, the famous Texan who had led the battle giving Texas its independence and had held power for many years, gave up and retired to his home in Huntsville. His son, Sam Houston, Jr., left Bastrop Military Institute to join the Confederate army in the first year of the war. After being taken prisoner while fighting in the Battle of Shiloh, young Houston was held prisoner for several months at Camp Douglas.

It was April 17, five days after the attack on Fort Sumter, when new Texas Governor Clark received the news. Immediately, he issued a call for volunteers. The dual job of furnishing soldiers for Texas' frontier protection and for the Confederate army posed a problem. Concerned that he could not provide enough men for two fronts, he sent a committee of Texas leaders to Montgomery to ask for help. The Texans were told to supply their own troops for both areas, because the war would not last long.

A sixteen-year-old Texan who enlisted in the Confederate Army

Soon, the new governor found there was no reason to be concerned about an insufficient number of troops. So many Texans enlisted that supplies of guns and ammunition grew scarce. Again, state officials appealed for Confederate aid—this time for arms. Unwilling to bypass any source, Clark asked merchants to transfer their stocks of gunpowder and bar lead to state leaders. He then encouraged Texans to set up gun and powder factories and sent agents to Mexico, Cuba, and Europe to buy more arms.

Once the war started, Texans who were against leaving the Union took various actions. A few joined the

Confederate army, because they did not want to fight against Texas. Others fled to Mexico and enlisted in the Union army. Some left Texas for other states or territories. Ones who remained at home either stayed neutral in action or formed secret societies to help the Union against the Confederacy.

One group of German settlers who had migrated to Texas to get away from war and political unrest decided to move rather than be involved in war. A company of Rangers sent to stop them caught them on the Nueces River. The settlers felt they had a right to move and resisted arrest. In the battle that ensued, several of them were killed or wounded.

Swen M. Swenson, the first Swede to settle in Texas, left because he feared for his life. Noted for establishing a number of successful businesses in Texas, he moved to New Orleans and set up operations in cotton and sugarcane. He later went on to New York to become a well-known banker and financier.

Some Texans who refused to accept secession worked to defeat Texas. Pro-Union men in San Antonio caused trouble throughout the war by celebrating Union victories and urging others to rebel against the Confederacy. In Central Texas, mass meetings protested Texans' being forced to join the army. The largest number of Pro-Union Texans was located in North Texas, where secret organizations were formed to cause unrest. One made plans to regain Union control by armed invasion. Others set up spy operations with people from the North and Confederate soldiers who were against secession. Rumors of other actions, often unfounded, spread throughout North Texas causing violence. Graveyards were robbed and destroyed; citizens unjustly accused of wrongdoings were placed in jail. Unruly mobs lynched over 40 men.

3

First Confrontation

During the secession convention, a Texas Committee of Public Safety was created. Ben McCulloch, a famous Texas Ranger and statesman, was commissioned military officer for the organization. His military career had started in Texas when he fought at the Battle of San Jacinto in charge of the "Twin Sisters," two small cannons donated by the people of Cincinnati, Ohio. His assignment now was to clear almost 3,000 Union troops scattered over several hundred miles of Texas frontier. His orders were to act immediately, because once Texas seceded, getting rid of Union troops could turn into a serious problem. So, almost two months before the Civil War started, Texans had their first confrontation with the Union army.

Benjamin McCulloch

It all began when Texas Rangers moved in to take over San Antonio. At the time, General David Twiggs was in command of the headquarters and supply depot in San Antonio. Born in Georgia, Twiggs was a

70-year-old who had started his military service in the War of 1812. Tall and distinguished looking, he had heavy white hair and a full white beard. A jewel-hilted sword in a golden scabbard, awarded to him by the U.S. Congress for gallantry in action, hung at his side.

During the night of February 15, 1861, McCulloch and his newly collected force of 1,000 volunteers began marching into San Antonio. Many had neither a uniform nor a horse to ride, but they were armed. As they came in, they marched to the town plaza carrying a Lone Star flag. By the next morning, the last of them had arrived.

When Twiggs, in the middle of a meeting, heard what was happening, he hurried outside. He was shocked to find troops already stationed around his headquarters at the Alamo. Aware that he had no way of stopping McCulloch with the 160 Union men stationed in San Antonio, Twiggs surrendered. Since war had not yet been declared, the Union soldiers were allowed to leave, unharmed, carrying food and weapons. McCulloch's men, elated over capturing San Antonio and $3 million worth of military equipment, started a big celebration.

General Twiggs surrendered the Union troops to the Confederate forces in the main plaza in San Antonio.

Robert E. Lee

In the midst of the Texans' victory, Robert E. Lee rode into San Antonio in an ambulance wagon. He was on his way to Washington after receiving orders to report immediately. For some time, Lee had been stationed in Texas. He was a lieutenant colonel at Fort Mason in charge of the cavalry.

Climbing out of the wagon in front of Read House, where he planned to spend the night, he was surprised to see crowds of men standing around in the streets. Some had strips of red flannel on their jackets showing they were officers. Lee could not understand what was happening. He met a friend in front of the hotel and asked what was causing all the excitement. When his friend told him that McCulloch had taken over army headquarters, tears came into Lee's eyes. He found a ride to the coast, where he boarded a steamer for home. Arriving in Washington on March 1, 1861, he met with several Union officers. They told him that Lincoln wanted him to lead the field command of the U.S. Army. Lee refused, asking, "How can I draw my sword upon Virginia, my native state?"

Lee left the meeting and rode back to his stately home, Arlington House, which sat on top of a hill overlooking Washington. He had lived there since his marriage to Mary Custis, great granddaughter of Martha Washington. Their wedding ceremony was held in the drawing room of the spacious home. Their seven children were born and reared at Arlington. He loved the United States and had served it for many years, but he would have to fight with his home state, Virginia. When he left to join the Confederates, his wife and family were driven from Arlington House by the Union army. The beautiful mansion and 1,100 acres of scenic lawns were converted into a cemetery.

Twiggs was also called to Washington where he was criticized for allowing McCulloch to take San Antonio without a fight. After being accused of "treachery to the flag," he was dismissed from the United States Army. Because he was sympathetic with the South, he joined the Confederates. For awhile he held a command in New Orleans but had to resign in 1862 because of ill health.

April brought drastic changes. On April 12, Confederate soldiers attacked Fort Sumter on the coast of South Carolina. Several issues brought the start of the Civil War, but a final one came when Union Major Robert Anderson moved his command from Fort Moultrie to Fort Sumter. Ordered to move back to Fort Moultrie, he refused. Continued refusal to leave Fort Sumter brought a Confederate ultimatum stating that firing would start in one hour. This refusal prompted the first shot of the Civil War on April 12 at 4:30 A.M. After 34 hours of battle, the Union surrendered, and the Confederates took over the fort. On April 15, Lincoln called for troops. Then four days later, on April 19, he ordered a blockade of all Southern ports from Virginia to Texas. The Civil War had begun, just as Sam Houston had predicted. The old warrior who fought for Texas' independence had fought again to prevent what he felt was a fatal mistake.

Unaware of what would come, Southerners were full of hope, even though they were handicapped in many ways. Trade with the North was cut off, but Confederates felt secure about importing supplies from foreign countries. For years, they had imported manufactured goods from England and France and had exported money-making crops of cotton, rice, sugarcane, and tobacco to the same countries. Feeling secure about plentiful supplies was short-lived, because the South was almost hopelessly outnumbered in too many ways.

The 23 states of the North had 22 million people, while the 11 states of the South had only nine million. Armed forces of the North greatly outnumbered those of the South. From the start, the South was also short of shipping and transportation facilities. The North's 30,000 miles of railways dwarfed the South's 2,000 miles.

Industries to produce ships, guns, and other needed war supplies were plentiful in the North, but the South had only two small gunpowder factories in its 11 states. Confederates had to struggle to get more military equipment. During the first two years of the war, blockade runners managed to bring over 300,000 supplies of arms and munitions through the blockade. Southern soldiers captured arms in several battles. In two conflicts alone, they took over 50,000 Union weapons. As the war progressed, the Confederates set up arsenals, foundries, and powder mills. Privately owned factories manufactured torpedoes, submarines, and cannons. Businesses were created to produce army clothing and shoes.

Despite extended efforts to provide for their armies, the Confederates would fall short, often lacking transportation to convey men and supplies to places where they were needed. In addition to a shortage of rail service, it became almost impossible for Confederates to buy horses and mules after horse-breeding regions of Tennessee and Kentucky were captured by the Union. With too few supplies available, many ragged, barefoot Confederate soldiers would die from exposure to cold. The lack of food would cause hundreds to lose their lives to diseases brought on by malnutrition.

4

Confederate States of America

On February 16, one week after he was elected, Jefferson Davis arrived in Montgomery, Alabama, a scenic little town perched on seven rolling hills beside the Alabama River. Housing facilities were scarce for newcomers. There were only two hotels, and both were crowded and not well kept. Since the capitol was too small to accommodate Confederate officials, the president had to hold office in a tiny hotel parlor. Other officers occupied a rented office building.

The new government was already formed. It had elected a president and vice president and had framed a constitution based on that of the United States, with only a few changes regarding such issues as state rights and slavery. Cabinet members were selected, and plans for the inauguration ceremony were set.

It was a cold, rainy day on February 18, 1861, when members of the Confederate government left the House of Delegates for the capitol. Led by a grand marshal, the band played "Dixie," a rousing song written by Daniel Decatur Emmett of Ohio and first played on Broadway in April, 1859. Behind the band, Jefferson Davis rode in a carriage along muddy, unpaved streets followed by Vice President Stephens and the cabinet. There was quite a contrast in the leaders' physical traits. Davis was over six feet tall; Stephens was short and weighed less than 100 pounds. Booming cannons fired salutes while 10,000 citizens gathered to watch. Davis stepped out of his carriage bareheaded, mounted a platform built in front of the capitol, and was sworn into a six-year term of office with the first Bible ever printed in the Confederacy. In his inaugural address, he stressed that secession was a right and reasonable step to take, because circumstances had made it a necessity rather than a matter of choice.

Davis took care to appoint members from different states to the new six-department cabinet. Even though Georgia lawyer and planter Robert Toombs had hoped to become president, he accepted the office of secretary of state. Later, he became so dissatisfied with Davis that he resigned and joined the Georgia militia as a brigadier general. Christopher Memminger, former governor of South Carolina, was chosen for secretary of the treasury. Leroy Pope Walker, leading Alabama secessionist, became secretary of war; much of the Confederate army's success came from his concentrated efforts to secure war materials. Former Florida Senator Stephen R. Mallory was chosen secretary of the navy. He stayed with Davis until the end. He was imprisoned by the Union and not released until March, 1866. Judah Philip Benjamin, a wealthy New Orleans lawyer and sugar planter, was appointed attorney general. He also stayed with Davis then escaped to England after the war. Texan John H. Reagan, chosen postmaster general, was a former frontier scout, Indian fighter, surveyor, and member of the Texas legislature and U.S. Congress. Staying with Davis until the end of the war, he was imprisoned then released in October, 1865. Reagan went back to Texas to practice law and later served again in the Texas legislature and the U.S. Congress.

Due to ill health, criticism, or disagreements with Congress, cabinet members changed constantly during the four years of the Confederacy. Benjamin was the sole cabinet member to serve as a replacement twice, and Mallory and Reagan were the only two who stayed in office until the war's end.

John Reagan did a remarkable job during his time in office and even made a profit for the new government. Required by the Confederate Constitution to be self-supporting after March 1, 1863, Rea-

John H. Reagan

gan closed small post offices, reduced the franking privileges allowing free postage for officials, made bargains with railroads on freight charges, and charged high postal rates. Then, eight months after Davis was inaugurated, the Confederacy issued its first stamps. They were colored green, carried a picture of Jefferson Davis, and were priced at five cents each.

A flag called the "Stars and Bars" was adopted. The flag's pattern was changed later, but at first it had a field of three horizontal bars, the outer two red, the inner one white, and a blue canton in the upper left corner containing a circle and seven stars. A later 13-star flag (instead of 11 showing the number of Confederate states) included Kentucky and Missouri. Even though these two states stayed in the Union, people of both states, in sympathy with the South, set up their own governments and attended the Confederate Congress.

Meanwhile, the last four states seceded. Virginia left the Union in April; Arkansas and North Carolina, in May; and Tennessee, in June, making a total of 11 states

"Stars and Bars" flag of the Confederacy

in the new country. Hampered by crowded conditions and lack of office space, government officials voted to move the capital to Richmond, Virginia, on May 21.

Spread over an area too large to be managed from Richmond, the Confederacy was divided into three districts. The one west of the Mississippi River was the Trans-Mississippi Department: made up of Texas, Arkansas, Louisiana, and Indian territory north and west of Texas. General Edmund Kirby Smith was placed in command of the area in February, 1863.

Kirby Smith, whose home state was Florida, was a graduate of West Point with many years of military experience. After fighting in the Mexican War, he returned to West Point to teach mathematics. In 1855, he was sent to Texas to serve in Indian campaigns. During the time secession was taking place, he was still in Texas in charge of Camp Colorado. When it appeared that war could not be avoided, he left Camp Colorado, resigned from the Union army on March 3, 1861, and joined the Confederates.

He served the first part of the war commanding troops in several areas east of the Mississippi River. After being wounded at Manassas, he was sent to Lynchburg to recover. There he met the woman who later became his wife. When he regained his health, he returned to battle command.

General Edmund Kirby Smith

A short time later, he received orders to report to the Trans-Mississippi area and set up headquarters at Shreveport, Louisiana.

When Vicksburg, the last point on the river still open to Confederates, fell to the Union on July 4, 1863, communication with Richmond headquarters became difficult. President Davis was forced to load Kirby Smith with heavy responsibilities. Davis ordered him to supervise the blockade crossing into Mexico; the sale of cotton to foreign nations; the smuggling of goods from Matamoros and Bagdad into Texas; and the factory operation where mines, powder, and guns were manufactured. His powers became so widespread that the department jokingly came to be called "Kirby Smithdom."

5

West of the Mississippi

After leaving San Antonio, Ben McCulloch was assigned to protect Indian territory west of Arkansas and south of Kansas. (Most of this land later became Oklahoma.) He was ordered to stop any invasion of these lands. First, he worked to win the help of Indians who had been given land there and other Indians who had been moved from Texas to the territory in 1859.

General Stand Watie

As part of a Confederate agency, he promised to continue aid that had been given them by the United States and also statehood if they would join the Confederacy. One of the Oklahoma Cherokee, Stand Watie, was the only Indian to become a Confederate brigadier general.

Watie, his regiment of Cherokee Mounted Rifles, and other Indian troops not only fought well to protect their territory but contributed many supplies to the Trans-Mississippi region. It was not unusual for the Indian general and his men to come out of a battle with many wagons loaded with supplies. In one raid alone, Watie and his troops captured 130 wagons loaded with supplies, took 135 prisoners, and killed or wounded over 200 enemy soldiers.

Ben McCulloch and his men were often called to work with other leaders west of the Mississippi River. When Sterling Price, governor and major general of Missouri, was unable to agree with important citizens of his state who insisted upon staying in the Union, he gathered an army, moved south, and set up camp. His army was composed of about 5,000 poorly armed men. Price soon learned that Brigadier General Nathaniel Lyon, working to rid Missouri of Southern believers, was advancing against him with 6,000 men. Quickly, he asked McCulloch for support. On August 10, 1861, Price, McCulloch, and their troops met the Union army near Springfield, Missouri, at Wilson's Creek. In the bloody battle that followed, both sides suffered heavy losses. McCulloch, in command, defeated the Union with 3,000 soldiers. Men who served under the famous Texas Ranger trusted in his leadership so strongly that they would follow him in anything he did.

A few months later when General Earl Van Dorn was ordered to take over military command of Missouri, he sent for Ben McCulloch to help. The two leaders, who had worked together in Texas, shared joint command of 16,000 troops. Over 3,000 of the soldiers were Indians from the Cherokee, Creek, Choctaw, Chickasaw, and Seminole tribes.

After organizing their men, McCulloch and Van Dorn left Arkansas traveling toward Missouri. On March 7, 1862, the two generals and their soldiers met the Union army at Pea Ridge in northwest Arkansas. During the fierce fight, McCulloch, leading one part of the army and

Van Dorn, leading another, were separated by bad roads. McCulloch disliked the Confederate gray uniform and was dressed in a suit of black velvet. The enemy spotted him easily. He was killed by a sniper's bullet. Robbed of the Ranger's brilliant leadership, his army lost spirit and was defeated. McCulloch's body was returned to Austin, Texas, and put to rest with honors in the State Cemetery.

After helping his brother occupy San Antonio, Henry McCulloch was sent to capture Union forts in northeastern Texas. Given command over the North Sub-District, he kept watch over that area and also fought in Arkansas, Vicksburg, and other areas of the borderlands.

After the McCulloch brothers took over San Antonio, another well-known Ranger, John S. Ford, was sent to Houston to gather volunteers. Most of Ford's friends and troops called him Rip. He got the nickname when, as a medical doctor in the Mexican War, Ford signed death certificates R.I.P. Ford. (R.I.P. stood for rest in peace.) After

John S. "Rip" Ford

Ford collected 500 men in Houston, he was ordered to drive the Union out of military posts along the Rio Grande. Leaving San Antonio short of food and arms, he and his men managed to defeat all Union posts along the way and gather food and supplies at the same time. The only place he was delayed was Fort Brown in Brownsville. The Union commander at the fort refused to surrender and even threatened to arrest Ford and his men. Ford left, gathered more men, then returned to capture the fort and all its arms and supplies.

Another famous group of Texas Rangers who fought west of the Mississippi was under command of Walter P. Lane. Lane came to Texas in 1836 and fought alongside Sam Houston, Ben McCulloch, and other Texas heroes in the Battle of San Jacinto. After Texas won its independence, he served as an Indian fighter and scout. During the war, he saw action in Arkansas with Ben McCulloch, then was ordered back to Texas to gather a cavalry regiment to fight in Louisiana. While leading troops in the battle at Mansfield, he was wounded and later appointed brigadier general.

Over 40 companies of other Texas Rangers were sent to guard the lands along the Red River. In addition to fighting with the Confederate army, these men had to keep constant watch over the Texas frontier where hostile Indian tribes often burned homes and crops and scalped and killed settlers.

Texas Rangers also continued to guard along the Rio Grande border in the area where Mexican bandits and outlaws often rustled cattle and stole wagonloads of goods being taken to Mexico to trade. One of the most famous of these outlaws was red-bearded Juan Nepomuceno Cortinas, who had many followers both in Mexico and Texas. Trouble with him started just before the beginning of the war and continued for months. On September 28, 1859, he started what came to be called the Cortinas War when he and his army attacked Brownsville, shot four men, and released all the prisoners from the Brownsville jail. Cortinas then set up quarters at Fort Brown for awhile before returning to his ranch at Matamoros. Later, when one of his men was arrested and jailed, Cortinas threatened to burn Brownsville to the ground if his man were not released. In the last few weeks of 1859 and first months of 1860, Cortinas was involved in several battles with Texans. One happened on February 4, 1860, when Rip Ford and his Rangers drove the famous bandit back to Mexico.

Robert E. Lee, who had served the United States in several crises, also played an important role in ending the Cortinas War. In March, 1859, Washington officials sent him to the Rio Grande to stop the violence. On his survey trip down the river, Lee met with Rip Ford. Ford, deeply impressed with the famous soldier, commented, "To approach him was to feel yourself in the presence of a man of superior intellect, possessing the capacity to accomplish great ends, and the gift of controlling and leading men."

6

Texans East of the Mississippi

Battles held east of the Mississippi River often had two names. Confederates named them after the nearest settlements or towns; the Union, after the nearest body of water. Fighting was light in the first year of the war but became increasingly heavy as the conflict progressed. The following chronologically traces the major battles of the war.

1861

April 12: Confederate troops attacked Fort Sumter.

July 21: Union troops retreated in disorder after the first Battle of Bull Run or Manassas.

1862

February 6: Union troops captured Fort Henry.

February 16: Union forces took Fort Donelson.

March 9: Two ironclad ships, Confederate *Merrimack* and Union *Monitor*, battled to a draw.

April 6–7: Union won the Battle of Shiloh; both sides suffered heavy losses.

April 18–29: Union fleet captured New Orleans.

June 6: Union armies captured Memphis.

June 25–July 1: Confederates under Robert E. Lee saved Richmond in Battles of the Seven Days.

August 29–30: Lee and Stonewall Jackson led Confederate troops to victory in the second Battle of Bull Run or Manassas.

September 17: Confederates were defeated in the Battle of Antietam or Sharpsburg.

October 8: Union stopped the Confederates' invasion of Kentucky in the Battle of Perryville.

December 13: Confederates crushed Union forces in the Battle of Fredericksburg.

December 31–January 2, 1863: Union forced Confederates to retreat after the Battle of Murfreesboro or Stone's River.

1863

May 1–4: Confederates defeated Union in the Battle of Chancellorsville.

May 1–19: Union defeated Confederates in Mississippi and started the siege of Vicksburg.

July 1–3: Union defeated Confederates in the Battle of Gettysburg.

July 4: Vicksburg fell to Union troops.

September 19–20: Confederates defeated Union in the Battle of Chickamauga.

November 23–25: Union armies were victorious in the Battle of Chattanooga.

1864

April 8–9: Confederates defeated Union troops in the Red River Campaign.

May 5–6: Confederates and Union troops clashed in the Wilderness Campaign.

June 3: Union suffered heavy losses in the Battle of Cold Harbor.

June 20: Union troops started the siege at Petersburg, Virginia.

July 11–12: Confederate forces almost reached Washington before having to retreat.

August 5: Union won the Battle of Mobile Bay.

September 2: Union captured Atlanta.

November 16: Hood's Confederates invaded Tennessee.

November 30: Union forces inflicted heavy losses on Hood's army in the Battle of Franklin.

December 15–16: Hood's army was completely defeated in the Battle of Nashville.

December 21: Union troops took over Savannah, Georgia.

1865

April 2: Confederates gave up Petersburg and Richmond.

April 9: Lee, who had become general in chief of the Confederate army on February 6, surrendered to Union at Appomattox.

April 26: Confederate Joseph Eggleston Johnston surrendered to Union Sherman.

May 4: Alabama and Mississippi Confederate forces surrendered.

May 26: The last Confederate troops east of the Mississippi River surrendered.

June 2: Kirby Smith and Magruder surrendered the Trans-Mississippi Department.

Several groups of the thousands of Texans who fought east of the Mississippi River became famous. Three of the most publicized Texas units were Terry's Texas Rangers, Hood's Brigade, and the Ross Brigade.

Terry's Texas Rangers were organized by Benjamin Terry. He moved to Texas when he was 20 years old and became a sugar planter. After serving as a delegate in the secession convention, he was sent to Virginia where he fought in the first Battle of Bull Run or Manassas. Confederates won the battle, but casualties were heavy. Southern losses numbered 387 dead, 1,582 wounded, and 13 missing. Northern losses were 460 dead, 1,124 injured, and 1,312 missing.

Discovering they were short of men, Confederate leaders sent Terry back to Houston, Texas, to gather more volunteers. Terry put out a call for troops who were to furnish their own arms and equipment for their

Two-thirds of Terry's Texas Rangers died fighting for the Confederacy.

horses. He collected 10 companies of 100 men who were formally placed under his command on September 9, 1861.

Two days later, Terry's men left Houston by railroads, riverboats, carts, and even some by foot. They met in New Orleans where they were invited to join General Albert Sidney Johnston in Bowling Green, Kentucky. Terry and his men quickly accepted the invitation after learning that Johnston was gathering an army to defend the frontier.

Johnston was a Kentucky-born West Pointer who had served with honor in many campaigns before moving to Texas. After moving, he enlisted in the state army as a private, but he quickly rose to the rank of senior brigadier general. At the end of his service in the Mexican War, he was assigned to Texas frontier duty. He helped lead the expedition escorting Mormons to Salt Lake City then was sent to California. When the Civil War started, Jefferson Davis appointed him to the rank of general.

After Terry's Texas Rangers became part of Johnston's army, they were constantly in action east of the Mississippi. They started with the Battle of Woodsonville in Kentucky late in 1861. Terry was killed leading a charge against Union troops on December 17, but his men continued to fight as a group through the rest of the war.

General Albert Sidney Johnston

Some of the battles in which they fought include the following:

Shiloh or Pittsburg Landing, Tennessee, April 6–7, 1862. (Shiloh was the name of a church on the battleground.) During the battle, General Johnston was shot in the knee. Despite his mens' pleas to get off his horse and stop fighting, he refused and bled to death. He was first buried in New Orleans but was later transferred to the State Cemetery in Austin. Johnston was considered by leaders of both the North and the South to be one of the most brilliant generals of the war.

Perryville, Kentucky, October 8, 1862. Weeks of drought in the area had dried up all the streams. Both Union and Confederate armies in the vicinity went to Chaplin Fork on the Salt River for water. There the two armies met in battle, bringing a loss of over 3,000 Confederates and almost 4,000 Union soldiers killed and wounded.

Murfreesboro or Stone's River, Tennessee, December 31, 1862. On the night before the battle, armies were camped so closely together that Union soldiers could hear the Confederates play "Dixie," and the Confederates could hear the Union's "Yankee Doodle." Casualties in the battle the next day amounted to about one-fourth of the South's troops and almost one-third of the Union's men.

Chickamauga River, September 19–20, 1863. (Chickamauga is the name of a river and a town in Georgia. The river, called "River of Death" by the Indians, runs into the edge of Tennessee.) The Confederates made most of the attacks and drove the Union back in this battle, which is known as the bloodiest in the war. Each army lost about one-third of its men. Sixteen thousand Confederates were dead or wounded and 2,000 were missing. The Union lost more than 11,000 who were killed or wounded and nearly 5,000 who were taken as prisoners.

Knoxville, Tennessee, November–December 4, 1863. Fierce battles and scattered fights on steep, icy slopes covered with deep mud ended on December 4. The results were heavy casualties and victory for the Union.

Another famous fighting group east of the Mississippi River was Hood's Texas Brigade commanded by John B. Hood. He was born in Kentucky but moved to Texas when he was very young. He claimed Texas as home. After graduating from West Point, he served in Missouri and California before being sent back to Texas to be stationed at Fort Mason and Camps Colorado, Cooper, and Wood. Part of his time in Texas was spent under the command of General Robert E. Lee.

The group was first organized in Richmond, Virginia, in the winter of 1861. Under the leadership of Texas lawyer Louis T. Wigfall, it was made up of several Texas regiments, a Georgia regiment, and a South Carolina infantry group.

When Wigfall resigned his command on February 20, 1862, to take a seat in the senate, Hood was placed in command, and the brigade was renamed Hood's Brigade. Later, it was split into two groups, with Hood taking charge of all Texas divisions. These Texans fought in about 24 major engagements. Some of the main conflicts were the

John B. Hood

second Battle of Bull Run, Antietam, Gettysburg, and Chickamauga.

Second Battle of Bull Run or Manassas, Virginia, August 29–30, 1862. Three Confederate generals—Lee, Jackson, and Longstreet—made a counterattack on Union forces. During the battle, Hood's men shoved the enemy back over a mile and captured four cannons. Casualties for the South were 9,000 men; for the North, 10,000.

Antietam or Sharpsburg, Maryland, September 17, 1862. Union General McClellan met Lee with about 90,000 men. The battle, one of the bloodiest of the war, was described by Hood as "the most terrible clash" so far. The brigade helped drive the Union back again and again, but the fight ended in Confederate withdrawal across the Potomac. Almost 11,000 Confederates, of which 560 were Hood's men, were either killed or wounded. The North suffered over 12,000 casualties.

Gettysburg, Pennsylvania, July 1–3, 1863. This conflict, called the greatest battle ever fought in the Western Hemisphere, happened accidentally. Shooting started when members of a Confederate cavalry were hunting shoes for barefoot troops and suddenly ran into Union soldiers. For three days the battle raged. Even though Hood's men were constantly on the defense, they reported that as fast as they ran through one line, another appeared. Running out of ammunition, Hood's men piled a rock wall on a hillside for protection. Because of the heavy losses—20,000 for the South and 17,000 for the North—Lincoln chose this site to deliver his famous Gettysburg Address. The president dedicated part of the battlefield to a cemetery, which later became a national military park.

Chickamauga River, September 19–20, 1863. On September 18, Hood's Texas Brigade and Terry's Texas Rangers joined other Confederates camped there.

Hood's Brigade went on to fight in losing battles at Chattanooga and the Wilderness campaign. During the Wilderness Battles in Virginia (May 5–6, 1864), Hood's men and other Texans were honored by General Robert E. Lee. On May 6, Lee was sitting on his horse watching his men being driven back by the quickly advancing Union army. Several hundred ragged young men raced up to Lee requesting orders. When he asked who they were, the young men answered that they were Texans. Lee shouted, "Hurrah for Texas!" and started forward to lead the attack. The young men yelled for him to come back. A Texas officer had to grab Lee's horse's reins to stop him while he was shouting, "Texans always move them!" A few minutes later, when Alabama soldiers asked Lee for orders, he pointed forward and said, "All I ask of you is to keep up with the Texans!" The South suffered 11,000 casualties; the North, 17,000.

This is the only known photograph of Hood's Brigade in the field.

On July 17, 1864, President Davis, displeased with the Department of Tennessee leadership, placed Hood in command. Now 33 years old, Hood was a distinguished looking man, even though he had lost the use of one arm at Gettysburg and had a leg amputated on the battlefield at Chickamauga.

Another band of fighting Texans east of the Mississippi was the Ross Brigade. Organized at Granada, Mississippi, in November, 1862, the brigade was first made up of four Texas cavalry units. Later, the Texans were combined with forces under General Earl Van Dorn. Then, on December 16, 1863, Lawrence Sullivan Ross assumed command of the brigade. He attended Baylor University in Waco and Wesleyan University in Alabama before becoming a Texas Ranger. While his father served as United States agent of the Brazos River Reservation near Waco, Ross gained valuable experience in dealing with Indians. During one Indian battle, he captured 34-year-old Cynthia Ann Parker, who had been taken by the Comanches when she was nine. At the beginning of the war, he resigned from the Rangers and entered the Confederate army as a private, but he quickly reached the rank of brigadier general. During his four years of war service, Ross fought in 135 engagements in Mississippi, Alabama, and Tennessee.

7

Dreams of Expansion: Sibley's Campaign

With thousands of Confederates already fighting both east and west of the Mississippi River, some Southern leaders were considering the start of another campaign. They dreamed of expanding the Confederacy across the west to California and the Pacific Ocean. When gold was discovered in California in 1848, the

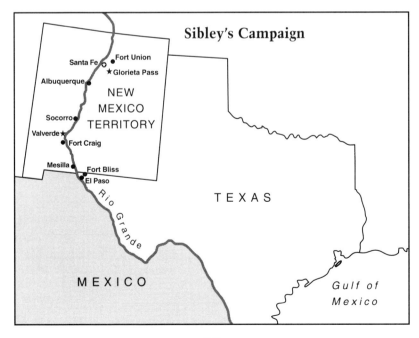

General Henry H. Sibley led a Confederate invasion of New Mexico.

state became very wealthy and established several ports on the Pacific. Leaders of the South believed that the people of California would gladly share their gold and ports with the Confederate States of America.

Henry Hopkins Sibley was one Southern leader who pushed for expansion. When the war first started, he was in the Union army stationed at Taos, New Mexico. On May 13, 1861, he resigned his commission and offered his services to the Confederates. Leaving New Mexico on June 12, he traveled to Richmond, Virginia, and met with Confederate leaders to propose a plan of westward expansion. Davis accepted Sibley's plan and commissioned him brigadier general.

Trained at West Point, Louisiana-born Sibley served part of his many years of military duty in both New Mexico and Texas. In addition to being a soldier, he was also an inventor. Four years before the start of the war, he designed a stove and a tent patterned after Indian wigwams. The United States Army used the invention for many years.

On July 8, 1861, President Davis issued Sibley's orders for the coming campaign: "In view of your recent service in New Mexico and knowledge of that country and the people, the President has entrusted you with the important duty of driving Union troops from that department, at the same time securing all army supplies and materials of war."

Further orders stated that he was to leave for San Antonio as soon as possible. General Earl Van Dorn, nephew of former President Andrew Jackson, graduate of West Point, and veteran of many military campaigns, would help him collect men, arms, and supplies.

Sibley arrived in San Antonio on August 12, set up headquarters, then issued a call for volunteer cavalry troops. Local newspapers cooperated by publishing articles asking volunteers to come to San Antonio immediately, armed and equipped for a winter campaign. Within two or three weeks, many Texans reported for duty. Weapons they brought included shotguns and fierce looking Bowie knives up to three feet long.

Sibley had no problem collecting troops without help from Van Dorn, but he ran into trouble trying to gather supplies. Shortly after Sibley had arrived in San Antonio, Van Dorn was transferred to Virginia. In his place came General P. O. Hebert, a former West Pointer stationed in Galveston. Unable to contact Hebert either, Sibley himself tried to collect as many supplies as could be spared from nearby army depots. Troop training started immediately.

While Sibley was meeting with Jefferson Davis, Colonel John Baylor, former Indian commissioner and member of the Texas Legislature, received orders to get started on the campaign. First, he was to take over Fort Bliss near El Paso. Then, after occupying the fort, he was to stage a surprise attack on the Union's Fort Fillmore, 40 miles north of El Paso.

Early in July, 1861, Baylor and his army seized Fort Bliss. After stationing troops there, he and about 250 men traveled up the Rio Grande toward Fort Fillmore, built near Mesilla in 1851. On the night of July 4, the Texans camped about 600 yards from the fort and prepared to

Colonel John Baylor

attack the next morning. But during the night, two of Baylor's men deserted and went to inform Union Major Isaac Lynde, commander of Fort Fillmore, about Baylor's plans. When Baylor heard about the deserters, he withdrew to Mesilla, only six miles away. The people there welcomed the Confederate soldiers with shouts of hurrahs.

The next morning, Baylor saw large clouds of dust moving across the plains toward Mesilla. He knew Lynde's Union troops were coming. Quickly, he arranged part of his men in battle formation and others on housetops and behind corrals. While they waited, women, children, and unarmed men went to the top of a nearby hill to watch. When the Union army arrived, Major Lynde spotted the people on the hill and commanded his men to fire upon them, but none of the watchers were hit. The major then ordered Baylor to surrender. Baylor refused to obey the orders, and the Union attacked. After three Union men were killed and six were wounded, the major ordered a retreat back to the fort.

Early the next day, Major Lynde and his troops set fire to the fort then left with all their supplies. They headed for Fort Stanton about 50 miles northeast of Mesilla. Baylor saw billowing smoke rising from Fort Fillmore and clouds of dust moving east and knew the fort was being abandoned. Quickly, he and his men pursued, but it was afternoon before they caught up with the Union army. Without a fight, Lynde surrendered his troops, arms, and supplies to the Texans leaving them in control of the Rio Grande. Five days later, on August 1, Baylor took formal possession of part of the New Mexico territory. He called it Arizona, named himself the governor, and made Mesilla the capital.

When Baylor completed setting up claim in Arizona and Sibley finished training his men, the two leaders met at Fort Bliss to combine troops. The combined group made a total of 3,700 soldiers.

Starting on October 21, 1861, with winter already setting in, Sibley sent one regiment at a time to camp a few miles below Fort Craig, a key site on the Rio Grande. Forts in New Mexico were different from those in Texas. Texas forts were made up of groups of buildings and tents laid out like a small village. Those of New Mexico were built for defense against attack, either surrounded by walls or by a square of buildings. Fort Craig was designed with several interior squares of buildings encircled by a four-sided enclosure also made of buildings. Erected on a flat area on the Rio Grande, it was surrounded by cottonwood trees and was noted as the prettiest fort in New Mexico.

Burdened with a wagon train, many cattle, and other supplies, the soldiers were forced to travel slowly. It was February 14, 1862, before all Texans reached camp. By then, many of them were ill with smallpox, which had broken out among Baylor's troops before Sibley's men arrived. Then, others caught pneumonia from being exposed to snow, sleet, and freezing temperatures without warm clothing and proper food.

In the meantime, Union Colonel E. R. S. Canby, commander of the Department of New Mexico and also

Sibley's brother-in-law, was moving troops to several sections of New Mexico. While Sibley's men marched toward Fort Craig, his brother-in-law was stationing part of his Union soldiers at the fort to stop the Texans.

By the time the Confederates reached camp, they were aware that Canby and his men were occupying Fort Craig and that it was heavily fortified. Rather than attack the protected position, Sibley and his officers decided to challenge the Union to a battle on open ground. Sibley, too ill to lead his army, placed Colonel Thomas Green in command.

Green was a capable leader. He started as a Virginia lawyer but after helping McCulloch fire the "Twin Sisters" at San Jacinto, he became a military man. Later, when he learned Santa Anna was being allowed to leave Texas on a Texas warship at Velasco, he went to Velasco, boarded the ship, and demanded that Santa Anna be returned to shore. Green fought against the Mexican leader again in the Mexican War.

Serving in Sibley's place, Green advanced his troops to an open plain near Fort Craig. Arriving there, the Texans held battle formation for hours. They tired of waiting and decided to leave; but while they were withdrawing, Canby's cavalry suddenly appeared and charged. When a small group of Texans, hidden in a nearby valley, opened fire with their cannons, Canby's men retreated back to the fort.

After Fort Craig troops refused to fight, the Texas army moved on toward Santa Fe, capital of New Mexico. Santa Fe, perched 6,950 feet above sea level is the highest capital in the United States. It was founded by Spaniards on the site of an old Pueblo Indian village in the year 1610.

Still traveling toward Santa Fe on February 21, Green and his men ran into Union troops at Valverde, a short distance north of Fort Craig. For hours, fierce hand to hand fighting took place. It was dark before the Union retreated and sent a flag of truce to the Texans. Sibley wrote to his superior officer that "For the first time, perhaps, on record batteries [cannons] were charged and taken at the muzzle of double-barreled shotguns, thus illustrating the spirit, valor, and invincible determination of Texas troops." Among the Union troops that day was Kit Carson, the famous scout, guide, and soldier known throughout the United States for his skills. When the war started, he was appointed colonel of the New Mexico Volunteer Regiment. After fighting at Valverde, he was sent to lead a campaign against Apache Indians and later had them placed on a reservation near Fort Sumner, New Mexico.

Three days later, another detachment of Texans reached Socorro, engaged in battle, and defeated the Union. Then all enemy supplies, including about 250 rifles and muskets, were captured. These weapons replaced the inferior lances the Texas cavalry had carried for weapons. Happy to get the guns but concerned about running out of food, the Texans pushed on toward Albuquerque. Scouts had reported that large food supplies were there. But before they reached there, the Albuquerque commander learned that the Texans were only 35 miles south. He quickly loaded food and military supplies in wagons, set fire to the buildings, and left for Santa Fe.

Some of the Texans moved in to occupy Albuquerque on March 7. They found themselves surrounded by cottonwood and willow trees. The Sandia Mountains loomed in the distance. After the Confederate flag was raised and a 13-cannon salute was sounded, part of the Texans moved on toward the capital.

By now, the Union officer in command of Santa Fe had heard that the Texans were on their way. Knowing he must find a safe place for the main body of stored supplies, he decided to take as much equipment as possible to Fort Union. One hundred twenty wagons were loaded, then two large warehouses of flour were burned. After cutting the flagpole down so Texans could not raise their flag, the Union men left. Two days later, the Texans reached Santa Fe and formally occupied it on March 13. Leaving troops to protect both Albuquerque and Santa Fe, several Texas units moved on toward Fort Union.

Sibley was pleased with the success his army had achieved against the enemy. His men had not only captured much needed arms and food supplies, but they had their enemy running. Now was the time to drive on to Fort Union, which Sibley considered to be the key area to the entire Territory of New Mexico. Fort Union was built in 1851 near Las Vegas, New Mexico, where many trails from the East met. (It would serve as headquarters and supply depot for the Union army for the next 30 years.) If the fort could be taken, the Texans' way westward would be open. The trail to Fort Union wandered through rugged territory. The army would have to start at Apache Canyon and follow the winding Santa Fe Trail through the southern end of the Sangre de Cristo Mountains. The long, seven-mile route was known as Glorieta Pass.

While the Confederates were busy seizing Albuquerque and Santa Fe, Canby was sending volunteer troops to Fort Union. Unknown to the Texans, part of the Union troops already at Fort Union were leaving to make a raid on Santa Fe. When Major Charles Pyron, Confederate leader at Santa Fe, learned these men were on the way, he and about 300 of his soldiers left to stop them. That night, the Texans camped at Johnson's Ranch near Apache Canyon.

The next morning, shortly after leaving the ranch, the Texans met Union soldiers bound for Santa Fe in the canyon. A fierce battle took place, and for the first time in the campaign, Sibley's men were defeated. After the fight, Pyron sent messages for help. Lieutenant Colonel William R. Scurry, a lawyer, former Austin newspaper owner, and well-known soldier, received one of the messages. Within 10 minutes, he and his men broke camp and left for Johnson's Ranch. At sundown, they were wading ankle deep in snow. By three o'clock the next morning, they reached Pyron and his men.

After a short rest, Scurry arranged the Texans in battle formation. By now, Colonel Tom Green, his men, and other detachments had arrived. All that day and night, the troops held their positions. Hour after hour passed, but no one came. Strained by the long watch, the Texans could wait no longer. If the enemy would not come to them, they would go to the enemy. Moving about six miles down the trail, the Texans met scouts hurrying toward them with a report that the enemy was just ahead. A short time later, the two armies met in a heated battle. After six hours, the fighting Texans routed the Union to claim victory in the Battle of Glorieta Pass on March 28, 1862.

The Texans' enthusiasm was dampened, though, when they returned to camp near Johnson's Ranch. Union soldiers had slipped in during the battle and burned their entire supply train of 73 wagons and killed over 500 horses and mules. With practically no food and ammunition, the men were forced to return to Santa Fe, 12 miles away. Back in Santa Fe, they sent a message to Sibley telling him what happened and asking him to send food and ammunition as soon as possible. They were ready to advance to Fort Union.

However, while they were waiting, a scout came to report that Canby and his men had left Fort Craig and were on their way to Albuquerque. The Texans immediately moved to help their men at Albuquerque. They had

Thirty-four Confederate Soldiers (ranging in age from 17 to 42) of the 4th, 5th and 7th Regiments of the Texas Mounted Volunteers were killed or died as a result of wounds during the Battle of Glorieta Pass, March 28, 1862.

The remains of thirty-one soldiers were originally interred in a mass grave on the New Mexico Battlefield at Glorieta Pass. After discovery of this grave on June 23, 1987, three soldiers were identified and reinterred in separate graves.

This monument honors the twenty-eight Confederate Soldiers who were reinterred here on April 25, 1993, and three others whose burial site remains known only to God.

FARRIER JOSEPH G H ABLE	2ND SERG JOHN H McKNIGHT
PVT RICHARD ALDAY	BLACKSMITH JAMES MANUS
PVT REUBEN F BENTLEY	2ND SERG STEPHEN MARBACH
PVT WILLIAM BOOKER	PVT JOHN R MARTIN
PVT EDWARD T BURROWES	PVT ALEXANDER MONTGOMERY
PVT EVERETT C FOLEY	PVT WILLIAM T PARSONS
PVT CHRISTOPH GOLLMER	PVT FRITZ SCHAEFER
1ST CORP BENJAMIN G GREELY	5TH SERG OTTO SCHROEDER
PVT AUGUST HABERMANN	PVT E R SLAUGHTER
PVT PETER HAIL	PVT JAMES R STEVENS
PVT JACOB HENSON	PVT BURTON R STONE
PVT F J HOPKINS	PVT WILLIAM STRAUGHN
PVT AUGUST JUHL	BUGLER G N TAYLOR
CORP WILLIAM LANGSTON	PVT ROBERT P WALKER
PVT JAMES McCORD	5TH SERG THOMAS D WILSON

PVT WILLIAM McCORMICK

PVT
EBINEEZER HANNA
CO C
4TH TX REGT
CSA
MAR 28 1862
BATTLE OF
GLORIETA PASS

PVT
J S L COTTON
CO E
4TH TX REGT
CSA
MAR 28 1862
BATTLE OF
GLORIETA PASS

barely arrived when they received another message that the army at Fort Union was on its way to join Canby and his men. This meant that Canby's entire army would arrive in Albuquerque. Knowing there was no way they could make a stand against the enemy without ammunition, the Texans had to retreat again.

Only one night after the Texans left, Canby's whole army did arrive in Albuquerque. Finding the Texans gone, the Union men followed them. In an effort to get away from the enemy, Sibley and his men traveled west to the San Mateo Mountains then turned south toward Fort Bliss. Sibley's men, many of whom were ill, had a hard time traveling along the sandy mountain trails. Many of their wagons sank into the unstable, soft soil. While the Texans were trying to dig them out, the Union caught up and captured all but seven of their 337 wagons, their weapons, and other supplies. Sibley's men struggled on without weapons and little food. Of the original force, only 1,500 troops were left when the tired, hungry, bedraggled army reached Fort Bliss.

On arriving at Fort Bliss, Sibley sent a discouraging report to headquarters. He wrote that New Mexico, except for its location, was not worth "a quarter of the blood" lost in the westward campaign. He continued that he and his men had beaten the enemy in every encounter and against large odds then ended the report with the opinion that it would be wise to "smother any hopes for a return to New Mexico." After a long wait with no answer from the state office, he and his men returned to San Antonio.

Baylor and his men were also forced to return to Texas. By late August, all surviving Texans were back home with dreams of westward expansion dismissed.

8

Blockade of the Texas Coast

While the Confederates were organizing armies and Baylor and Sibley were starting their expansion westward, the Union naval blockade was moving slowly toward Texas. It had a long way to go to cover the South's almost 3,500 miles of seacoast from Virginia to Texas. At the beginning of the war, the Union had only 42 active ships. Twenty-six were steamers. The others were sailing vessels. Many more had to be added as the war progressed. By December, 1864, the Union had 671 vessels, including 71 ironclads. At the start of the war,

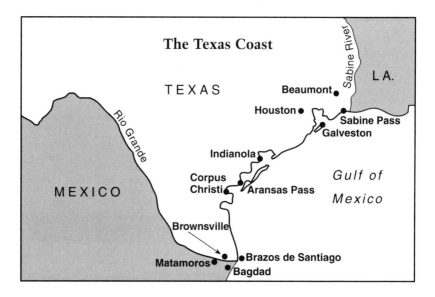

personnel in their navy totaled only 7,400. By the end, the number had risen to 68,000.

Skipping many ports along the way, part of the Union navy reached Texas during the summer of 1861. At that time, the Texas coast had no defenses. Hurriedly, slaves were put to work fortifying the ports and inlets at Galveston, Sabine Pass, Matagorda, Aransas Pass, and Port Isabel.

In August of 1862, about the time Sibley's men returned to Texas, the Union navy was reinforced with more vessels. Almost immediately the ships were put into action attacking Matagorda Bay and Corpus Christi. Even though both attacks were halted, Corpus Christi suffered damage from the bombardment. One month later, Union men struck Sabine Pass. They destroyed the fort and the bridge to the mainland then moved north to Beaumont where they inflicted serious damage.

General Kirby Smith knew that it would not be long before an attack would be made on Galveston. As early as 1825, the Galveston area had been recognized as a perfect gateway into the interior of Texas. Stephen F. Austin sent settlers there in 1836 to open a post office and custom house. Then, when wharves were built out into deep water of the bay, Galveston became an official port. It grew fast to become one of Texas' main cities and by 1853 had three railroads connecting the port with the mainland.

Kirby Smith sent orders to Brigadier General Paul Hebert to reinforce Galveston's defenses. Even though Hebert was a graduate of West Point, he had spent much time in Europe where he had been influenced by foreign military styles. Some Texas leaders thought he was a bit too arrogant and headstrong.

Hebert started by fortifying the few small defenses already constructed in the port. Earthen embankments were piled around the city, and small forts were created that would guard the channel leading in from the bay. Single-gun posts protected with armor plate were placed within the city on Ninth, Fifteenth, and Twenty-first streets. The three railroads leading into the city were protected by four mounted cannons. The railroads, together with a telegraph station, were the only means of communication with the mainland.

On October 4, 1862, the expected attack came. Union Commander William B. Renshaw entered Galveston harbor, raised a flag of truce, and demanded that the city surrender. Galveston's commander, Joseph J. Cook, refused. Cook was a graduate of the U.S. Naval Academy and a dedicated officer. His second job was serving as a part-time Methodist preacher, but he was ready to fight to hold Galveston. He asked for truce time to send families and children to the mainland. He was given four days.

The four days, somehow, stretched into a longer period. It was not until Christmas Day of 1862 that the Union navy actually moved into the city. Landing at the harbor, almost 300 men barricaded themselves at the end of Twentieth Street on Kuhn's Wharf.

Galveston offered a gateway into the interior of Texas.

Over Cook's frantic objections, headstrong Hebert announced that there were not enough men and supplies to fight the enemy and surrendered. Galveston was captured without a fight. When Union Rear Admiral David Farragut received news of the surrender, he was elated. He exclaimed that now the Union had secured nearly the entire coast of Texas without losing one man. Later, he would regret saying these words.

Farragut was Union commander of the Western Gulf Coast, which included Texas. A Southerner born in Tennessee, he was 60 years old but still agile enough to do handstands. He had already served 50 years of military duty. When he was only 10 years old, he held a job as a midshipman fighting through the War of 1812. Later, he battled pirates in the West Indies, then fought in the Mexican War. Farragut was an experienced officer, but he would meet his match in Kirby Smith.

Knowing the Union would use Galveston as a base for moving inland to occupy Texas, not only Cook, but other Confederate leaders were shocked to learn Hebert had surrendered without a fight. Immediately, Hebert was replaced with Colonel John Bankhead Magruder. A Virginia West Pointer, Magruder had served the United States in many areas. After fighting in the Seminole and Mexican Wars, he was stationed at various times in California, Maryland, and Rhode Island. When the Civil War started, he resigned from the Union and became a colonel with the Confederates. He proved to be a fine officer in several battles east of the Mississippi, but then he made several serious errors while fighting in the Shenandoah Valley. On October 10, 1862, he was transferred across the Mississippi River to Texas.

After reaching his new command, Magruder's first job was to run the Union out of Galveston. To recapture Galveston, though, he needed ships, and Texas had very few. In fact, the only available ones were actually small steamers used for carrying mail and supplies on rivers in bay areas. Texas once had a small navy of four boats when it was a republic. However, so many problems developed with the little steamers that Sam Houston tried to get Congress to sell them. When many Texans objected to losing their navy, the sale was called off. Later, after Texas became a state, the little steamers were transferred to the Union.

In addition to having few steamers, there was a shortage of artillery. The few cannons available were old, damaged, and worn out. Refusing to be held back by a lack of equipment, Magruder, helped by former California sea captain Commodore Leon Smith, organized a Texas navy. (Smith was reported to be the brother of one of Lincoln's cabinet members.) Even though there were only six small boats, this navy became known as Magruder's Fleet. Since there was no protection on these vessels, the decks were lined with bales of cotton, bringing a new name, "cotton-clads." Ammunition used in the few old guns mounted on the cotton-clads was referred to as Magruder's Pills. For added weapons, the men had an assortment of rifles, shotguns, Bowie knives, and swords.

Colonel John B. Magruder

When Magruder started organizing troops, Tom Green and William Scurry, back home from Sibley's campaign, came to fight. Tom Green brought about 200 of his sharp-shooting cavalrymen. Other welcomed recruits were the Davis Guards, named after Jefferson Davis. All of the guards were Irish, chosen for their toughness and bravery. They later earned the name "Fighting Irishmen."

One young Davis Guard would play a leading part in the coming coastal battles. His name was Richard William (Dick) Dowling. Born in Ireland, he was brought to America by his family, who was fleeing the potato famine in the 1840s. In New Orleans, he lost his mother and father in a yellow fever epidemic. At that time, this disease, carried by mosquitoes, was common throughout Central America and the Gulf Coast region. After Dowling grew up, he moved to Houston, where he set up a business in October, 1857. He married an Irish girl, Elizabeth Ann Odlum, the next month. His business, a club for men, prospered. It was the first saloon in Houston to install gas lights. A year later, in 1858, he became a citizen of the United States. Dowling joined the David Guards in 1860 as an artilleryman. Commanded by Fred Odlum, the uncle of Dowling's wife, the Davis Guards also enlisted Dowling's brother, Patrick, and his brother-in-law, Edward.

With ships and troops gathered, Magruder turned his attention to communication. He and Commodore Smith

Elizabeth Ann and Dick Dowling

stationed a detachment of cavalry scouts along the coast to keep in constant touch with movements of the Union navy. Any information gathered was either taken to headquarters or sent by telegraph, a fairly new service in several areas of Texas. Magruder was thankful for the telegraph but did not intend to depend wholly upon it. He came up with the idea of using civilians in small boats, posing as peddlers, to spy on movements of Union troops holding Galveston.

From the scouts and spies, Magruder learned that only three companies of soldiers were on guard in Galveston and that Union ships were docked at the end of Kuhn's Wharf. He also found that there were five large ships and several small boats. All were armed. With men, equipment, and information collected, Magruder and Smith set January 12, 1863, as the day to start attacking Galveston.

In the meantime, a slave cook escaped from one of the Texas camps. He went to Galveston and told Union leaders that Magruder planned to attack on January 12. Fortunately for the Texans, there was a Southern woman, Mrs. Rosanna Osterman, who used her home in Galveston as a hospital to treat soldiers. She learned from a Union patient in her hospital that the enemy now knew of the Confederate plans. She also heard that more Union troops were on their way to Galveston to occupy Houston and other inland areas of Texas.

Quickly, Mrs. Osterman sent one of her trusted slaves with a message to Commodore Smith. At that time, he and a unit of troops were at Virginia Point on the mainland opposite Galveston. When Smith received the message, he immediately went to Houston to notify Magruder. Together, the two men decided to set an earlier time for the attack in order to surprise the enemy. New Year's Day, 1863, was chosen for invasion time.

9

Recapture of Galveston

Just two hours before New Year's Day of 1863, Magruder and his men started across the two-mile bridge joining Galveston with the mainland. Land troops, under the command of General Bill Scurry, pushed heavy artillery over a railroad track.

While walking across, Magruder thought it was strange that no enemy guards were posted around. Quietly, he led his troops into the city and positioned them around Kuhn's Wharf at the end of Twentieth Street. He was surprised to find the planking on the wharf had been removed and a barricade of heavy timbers had been constructed to shield the Union ships. His plans had been to send some of his men across the wharf to attack the ships. With no planking, though, his troops would have to wade through water carrying ladders to scale the barricade. Magruder knew it would be a dangerous move, but there was no other way.

Texans on shore would not start firing until their two cotton-clads, the *Bayou City* and *Neptune*, carrying General Tom Green and his sharpshooters, arrived to help them. The cotton-clad steamers, with prows protected by an iron covering for ramming, were supposed to have reached Galveston at the same time the troops did, but they were late. Success in the coming battle depended

The Battle of Galveston

upon striking in the dark before the enemy could spot the Texans' positions.

Magruder, Scurry, and their men waited. It was five o'clock in the morning, but the cotton-clads were still not in sight. If there were enough light to see, the two big Union warships at the end of the wharf were near enough to shoot down most of the Texas troops. Aware it would be daylight before long, Magruder realized that he must attack without the help of the *Bayou City* and *Neptune*. He fired the first cannon himself. The other cannons followed. Immediately, answering blasts came from the Union ships, the *Harriet Lane* and the *Owasco*, sitting close to the wharf.

The Texans' first shots made holes in the barricade at the end of the wharf. Magruder's troops, many of whom were Davis Guards, leaped into the icy water and waded to the barricade standing between them and the ships. Reaching there, the men discovered that their ladders were too short to climb over. Weighed down by water-soaked clothing, the Texans turned and struggled back to shore amid heavy fire from the enemy ships. Dawn came bringing enough light to expose the land troops' positions. With more and more Texans being hit by artillery fire, Magruder and Scurry ordered their men back toward the city. Just as they retreated, the two little cotton-clads steamed into the harbor.

The captains aboard the *Bayou City* and *Neptune* saw three Union ships out in the bay. So they headed toward the *Harriet Lane* and the *Owasco*, harbored closest to the wharf. Amid the roar and smoke of heavy artillery fire, the two little cotton-clads headed directly at the *Harriet Lane*. The Texans intended to ram the warship but missed. As they turned to make another pass, the *Neptune* was hit. Drifting to one side, it sank and settled in the mud, leaving the *Bayou City* to fight alone.

Armed with only one cannon, the little steamer made another pass. This time, it rammed straight into the heavily armed *Harriet Lane*, locking onto its side. Now at close range and sheltered by thick bales of cotton, Green and his sharpshooting Texans riddled the deck of the Union ship with rifles and shotguns. When many men aboard the warship were wounded or killed, the rest of the Union crew retreated below deck.

In the meantime, the one cannon on the *Bayou City* was hit. It blew up, killing Captain A. R. Wier and several other men. Before the cannon was destroyed, though, one shot from it hit the *Owasco* and killed its captain and many of its sailors. So, now, one Union warship was out of action.

On the wharf, heavy fighting was going on between Union troops and the Texans. Green and his sharpshooters, aboard the little cotton-clad, continued firing their rifles and shotguns without stopping. In the midst of flying shells, Commodore Smith leaped from the *Bayou City* to the deck of the *Harriet Lane* shouting, "Cowards won't follow me!" Every man on the *Bayou City* jumped right behind him. Once on the big ship, they engaged in heavy hand-to-hand fighting. Union soldier Jonathan M. Wainwright (reported to be of the same family as the famous World War II general of the same name) was killed during the fight.

Seeing that their two ships by the wharf were in trouble, the three Union vessels in the bay moved in to help, with the *Westfield* in the lead. Amid the smoke and noise of battle, Commodore Smith sent a message to the *Westfield's* Commander Renshaw, "If you don't stop firing on us, I'll massacre everyone on board the *Harriet Lane*." Commander Renshaw, Union leader in the capture of Galveston, was chief officer aboard the *Westfield*. He agreed to surrender and sent word to Union soldiers on the wharf to yield to Magruder.

The agreement had hardly been reached when it was broken. Renshaw ordered all Union ships to leave. The *Clifton*, the *Sachem*, and the *Owasco* turned and steamed from the harbor. Suddenly, the *Westfield* was caught on a mud flat and could not move. Renshaw ordered a delayed fuse lit in the magazine of his ship to destroy it before the Texans could capture it. While his men were leaving the vessel, the fuse ignited too quickly, and many Union men were killed, including Commander Renshaw.

The battle for Galveston was over, giving the Texans control of their main port again. Casualties were heavy for the Union, with about 200 men killed and about 400 prisoners taken. Only 12 Texans lost their lives, and 143 were wounded. The Texans scored a satisfying victory and captured many valuable supplies. Houston sightseers aboard a yacht watched as a Union ship and two small sailing boats loaded with Irish potatoes were taken.

Like other periodicals of the South, the *Houston Tele-*

graph, Texas' foremost newspaper, was suffering from a paper shortage. Often, wallpaper or wrapping paper served as a substitute for newsprint. Despite the shortage, the *Houston Telegraph* ran a long article about the battle and gave special praise to the Davis Guards.

Throughout the rest of the war, Confederates controlled the island.

10

The Ghost Called *290*

Afew days after the Battle of Galveston, the Union blockade was strengthened with five more warships. On January 11, 1863, officers aboard the new vessels saw a strange ship approaching. Union Commodore Henry H. Bell, who helped Farragut command the Texas blockade, suspected it was a blockade runner. He sent the *Hatteras* to pursue it, but his ship soon disappeared from view. Bell waited and waited. When his ship did not return, he sent another to look for it. The second one found the *Hatteras* sunk in the Gulf of Mexico with nothing but its masts showing above the water.

A few sailors who escaped the sinking vessel were found in a small lifeboat. They told Commodore Bell that the ship they had followed was not a blockade runner. It was a heavily armed Confederate vessel called the *Alabama*, which had defeated the Union ship in a 13-minute battle despite the Union ship's being larger by 100 tons. The captain of the *Hatteras* and all his men except the few who escaped in the small boat were taken prisoners.

The *Alabama* had been built just one year before in Birkenhead, England. It was nicknamed the *290*, because it had been the 290th ship built by the British company. Since England was neutral, American ships bearing arms

C.S.S. Alabama #290

could not be built there while the war was still in progress. But Captain Raphael Semmes, commander of the *290*, had already made arrangements to have arms installed on his new ship after leaving England. The vessel left England and sailed straight to the Azores, a group of islands west of Portugal. A ship loaded with weapons was waiting. The two vessels were lashed together while arms were transferred to the *Alabama*. This new 220-foot long wooden vessel weighed 1,000 tons. It had sails and two engines so that it could move either by sails or by steam. Now that it was armed with eight guns, it would cause much damage to Union trading and transport vessels.

Semmes had been in the U.S. Navy for a long time. When the Civil War started, he followed his home state, Alabama, and joined with the Confederates. His initial command was aboard the *Sumter*, the first warship owned by the Confederate navy. It had been converted from a steamer to a warship in New Orleans. Within six months, Semmes and his men captured 18 Union trade ships, but the *Sumter* was blockaded at Gibraltar by the Union navy and had to be abandoned.

His next command was aboard the *290* with a crew of almost 150 men. Goods were captured from several Union ships near the Azores and on the north route to Newfoundland. Newspapers among the booty taken from one ship reported that Union General Banks planned to invade Texas at Galveston.

Semmes set out south to Galveston where he could help stop the Union by taking their ships and supplies. But by the time he reached there, Magruder and his army had already shoved the Union out of their main port. So he attacked the only ship that pursued him and left for Jamaica. On reaching Jamaica, he freed the *Hatteras* prisoners, refueled his ship, and sailed down to Brazil. Leaving Brazil, he sailed across the South Atlantic, around the Cape of Good Hope, crossed the Indian Ocean and South China Sea, then came back to the Atlantic. He and his men almost stopped Union trade in the areas where they traveled.

After cruising for two years over 75,000 miles of water, the *Alabama* was badly in need of repairs. On June 11, 1864, Semmes entered the port of Cherbourg, France. While he was waiting for permission from the French government to have his ship repaired, the Union warship *Kearsarge* steamed into port. Semmes sent a message to the captain of the Union ship challenging him to a duel.

On Sunday, June 19, the two ships, observed by many spectators on the coast, moved a short distance from the port. When the *Alabama* opened fire, shells dropped away from the sides of the *Kearsarge*. Hidden under the wood planking were heavy metal chains, which could not be seen. Return fire from the Union warship sank the *290*.

Unaware that the *290* left the Gulf after sinking the

Hatteras and would never return, men of the U.S. Navy lived in fear of meeting it again. Time after time, Farragut received reports that the *290* had been sighted in the Gulf of Mexico. He came to think that it must be on constant patrol and issued a warning to all captains of his ships to travel in groups of three. The admiral felt it would take at least this many of his armed vessels to handle the *290* in battle.

Whether U.S. naval men were seeing ships that looked like the *290* or had a ghost of the dreaded vessel in their minds was never determined. But they never stopped sending reports to Farragut that they had seen the *290*. Oddly enough, several months after the sinking of the *Hatteras*, fear of the *290* would play a role in the defeat of the Union at the Battle of Sabine Pass.

11

Surprise at Sabine Pass

Sabine Pass, bordered on the east by Louisiana and on the west by Texas, served as an outlet to the Gulf of Mexico for two rivers. Both the Neches and Sabine Rivers flowed into Lake Sabine, which was about 10 miles wide and 25 miles long. At the end of the lake was the narrow channel, Sabine Pass. The upper part of the pass was split into two separate channels by a wide oyster bed.

In 1859, two years before the start of the war, Sabine City, inland from the pass, was a thriving port. That year over 300 ships had been in and out of the port. About 100,000 barrels of merchandise were imported, as well as cotton, building materials, and cattle. The little town had a church and several businesses, including a saw mill, a weekly newspaper, an insurance company, and a large hotel.

Fort Griffin was built on the Texas side, a half mile south of Sabine City. Badly damaged now, the fort had the remains of an earthen wall eight feet high and 12 feet thick on the south, east, and west. The north side at the rear had a wall only four feet high. Two miles southeast of the fort sat a deserted lighthouse towering 85 feet into the air.

After the Battle of Galveston, Magruder decided Fort

Griffin was too important to be abandoned. He sent Captain Fred Odlum and his Davis Guards to "clean up the place," which had been almost destroyed by the Union several months before. The fort needed more than cleaning up.

After surveying the placement of the fort, the Guards decided to move it farther inland from the mouth of the pass. For added protection, they shoveled tons of dirt to form higher embankments on the three sides facing the Gulf of Mexico. At the rear, more soil was piled on the four-foot earthen wall. Dowling and several of his men placed large poles out in the channel at the closest place the enemy could bring ships. They practiced shooting at the poles often. This spot, 1,000 yards from the fort, would prove to be a deadly location for some Union ships. Magruder sent additional equipment of two old steamers, the *Josiah H. Bell* and the *Uncle Ben*, which had been converted into gunboats.

For quite a while two Union blockaders, the *Morning Light* with nine guns and the *Velocity* with two guns, had kept watch on the pass, stopping all trade that had formerly slipped through. Troops at Fort Griffin were given orders to drive them away. Early on the morning of January 21, 1863, the guards and about 250 other men boarded the *Uncle Ben* and the *Josiah H. Bell*. The only heavy gun carried was aboard the *Josiah H. Bell* and was manned by Dick Dowling. It was a 64-pounder with an eight-inch barrel bored like a rifle. Some called it "The Magruder," but the Davis Guards named it "Annie" in honor of Dowling's wife. Four other weapons in such bad shape that they could not be fired, were carried to impress the enemy.

Just before daylight when the Texas cotton-clads steamed out into the Gulf of Mexico, the blockaders were directly in front of them. Both of the Union ships were much larger than the Texas boats and were heavily armed. To the Texans' surprise, the Union vessels turned and ran. Dick Dowling, unable to understand why they were leaving, decided to chase them. Later in the morning, Dowling came within firing range of the *Morning Light* and fired two shells. A third one jammed, but his steamer moved on while he dislodged the shell. With the barrel clear, he continued to fire and hit the Union ship many times. One shell exploded on its deck.

Moving even closer to the big ship, the Texas sharpshooters opened fire. Union men tried to fire back from the cabin on deck but had to retreat below. Finally, the commander of the Union ship surrendered. Dowling turned his gun on the *Velocity* and forced it to give up also.

After the surrender, Dowling led some of his men onto the *Morning Light*. He found that the magazine was flooded, and he ordered the Union prisoners to pump it dry. Then, the two little steamers towed both Union ships back to Sabine Pass. Unable to move the *Morning Light* through the pass, the guards burned it, but the *Velocity* was saved. One hundred nine prisoners, 11 cannons, 150 small guns, and other supplies worth $100,000 were captured. While supplies were being unloaded at the fort, several Union gunboats were sighted in the Gulf of Mexico. Hurriedly, Dowling and his men left the *Morning Light*. The two small Texas boats were fired upon as they steamed away, but they only suffered a little damage, and no Texans were wounded.

When Farragut received a report that two small Texas steamers had captured his ships, he was furious. His men had to find a way to stop those Texans from attacking Union blockaders and slipping through the Union blockade.

Cotton was traded for weapons in Mexico.

President Lincoln continued to receive reports that Texans were trading cotton for weapons and supplies through Mexico. Continued trade was being made possible through the efforts of the Texas State Military Board, created in January, 1862, when the blockade first neared Texas. After attempts to sell bonds to sustain foreign trade failed, the board turned to the cotton trade to provide finances and weapons. Difficulty in transporting cotton to Mexico was overcome when the agency created a route that started at Brownsville, went across the Rio Grande to Matamoros, Mexico, and down to Bagdad, a Mexican port at the mouth of the river. Since Bagdad belonged to Mexico, it was protected from Union trade interference by international law.

In agreement with Farragut, Lincoln insisted that action be taken to stop the Texas cotton trade, because it was not being halted by the blockade. Conferring with his military leaders, he found that each had a different opinion about a suitable location for invasion. Some favored the Red River while others wanted to use the Rio Grande. Some said Galveston would be best. Others declared Indianola was the key spot.

Finally, Lincoln sent a message to Union General Nathaniel Banks to take action now and to make the decision on a starting point for the invasion. Banks, a former lawyer, legislator, and Massachusetts' governor, was commander of the Union Department of the Gulf. He, too, was undecided on a penetration point. Meeting with Farragut to hear his opinion, Banks learned that the admiral favored Sabine Pass.

Farragut explained that he thought the Union had been underestimating the importance of the little port. He had information that large amounts of munitions and other supplies entered Texas at Sabine Pass and that enormous loads of cotton left from there. Then, too, after an invasion, it would be easy to go on to Beaumont, 30 miles northwest by rail, and continue on to Houston, the railroad center of Texas. Cotton worth millions of dollars was reported to be stored there, and taking over the rest of Texas from that point would present no problem.

In the coming invasion, Farragut wanted the army and navy to work together. Army and navy leaders met to discuss a plan for attack. Entering Fort Griffin from the front could only be accomplished on water, but moving ships through the low water and mud flats of the pass leading to the fort could be difficult. Army leaders suggested that the best plan was for the navy to take army troops to a beach a couple of miles from Sabine Pass. Once landed, the troops could move around to the unprotected rear of the fort to start the attack. General Banks agreed with this plan except for one point. The troops would need covering fire when they landed and moved to the rear of the fort.

Banks' next step was to talk with the navy about providing ships for the invasion. He asked for enough vessels to carry 20,000 troops for the first landing at Sabine Pass but learned that there were only enough available to transport 5,000 or 6,000 men. There was a shortage due to the amount of ships being used on the Mississippi River and in the blockade of the Confederate coast.

Then, also, a special type of vessel was needed for the invasion. The ships had to be sturdy enough to make the trip from New Orleans to Sabine Pass in the rough waters of the Gulf. They had to be large enough to carry several thousand men, arms, and other supplies, but light enough to pass over the shallow waters and muddy sandbars in the pass.

A long-time whaleship captain, Frederick Crocker, was chosen to command the ships collected for Banks. Crocker had been in the navy for several years but had resigned. In 1862, the navy persuaded him to come back. One of his assignments early in the war was to lead a raid on Sabine Pass. Since he was already familiar with the dangerous crossing from the Gulf of Mexico into the pass, the navy felt he was an ideal leader for the invasion. Crocker's flagship was the *Clifton*. Gunships *Sachem* and *Arizona* would provide support for him. Major General William Franklin, who fought against Magruder in the Battles of the Seven Days in Virginia, would direct the army landing then move on to the Beaumont to Houston railroad. After the landing, General Banks would take command.

One day before the actual attack, plans called for a fast ship to carry a message to blockade ships off the shore of Sabine Pass alerting them to the attack time. After delivery was completed, the ship would anchor at the mouth of the channel as if it were another blockade vessel. Its most important task would be to shine a bright light on the night of September 6, 1863, to show the fleet where to anchor. Then, early on the morning of

September 7, under cover of darkness, the messenger ship would guide the fleet through the channel for a surprise attack on the fort.

During the attack, while the gunboats were firing on the fort, the Union infantry, artillery, and cavalry could land on the beach unnoticed. While the battle was in progress, some of the heavy gunboats were to guard the Gulf side of the pass should the dreaded *290* come to help the Texans. The Union still watched for this feared ship, unaware that it was halfway across the world and would never return.

Three or four days before the start of the invasion, a fourth gunboat, *Granite City*, was added to the Union fleet. It would act as the messenger ship carrying first instructions to vessels waiting outside the pass. Its length was 160 feet, its weight 450 tons, and it had two engines and two boilers to give it adequate speed.

The captain of this vessel was a former Massachusetts ship captain by the name of Charles W. Lamson. Poor Lamson harbored a deep fear of meeting the *290*. When he learned that he would not have armed escorts while serving as messenger, he was even more alarmed. Farragut's warning that at least three gunboats were needed to fight the dreaded ship kept coming to Lamson's mind. Even though the *Granite City* was armed with four howitzers, one pivot gun, and 30 army sharpshooters, Lamson's worry grew.

12

Delay of Invasion

Despite carefully laid plans for the invasion, a series of mishaps began to take place. The operation was to start late on Sunday, September 6. That Sunday only one ship, the *Owasco*, commanded by Lieutenant Commander Madigan, was on duty blockading Sabine. Madigan had been given command after the ship's former captain was killed in the Battle of Galveston.

On the afternoon of September 6, the commander discovered his supply of engine oil was low. Having no other vessel near to help him, he left his post and headed for the Union blockade fleet off the coast of Galveston to pick up more oil. Reaching there about 3:30 P.M., he loaded barrels of oil from the Galveston ships then left for Sabine at 8:00 P.M. (He had not received the message about invasion plans for that night.)

While Madigan was gone, the *Granite City* arrived at Sabine Pass late in the afternoon. Lamson was surprised then alarmed when he found no blockade ships. While waiting, he thought he saw a large gray gunboat in the distance. Fearing it was the dreaded *290*, he left.

Two days before this time, four Union ships had left New Orleans. Escorted by the *Arizona*, they were carrying General Godfrey Weitzel and over 1,000 troops to Sabine. General Weitzel was a West Point graduate who had much experience in infantry marsh warfare in Louisiana, the same type of land they would find at Sabine. Meanwhile, 18 more Union ships were on their way down the Mississippi River to enter the Gulf at New Orleans. Plans called for them to be just a few hours behind General Weitzel, but they were running late and did not reach the Gulf until late on September 6. There were still many miles to travel before reaching Sabine.

Two of the Union ships, the *Clifton* and the *Sachem*, finally caught up with Weitzel and his vessels about halfway from New Orleans to Sabine Pass. The ships moved on together led by the *Clifton*. This ship, a 210-foot long steamer, had been chosen flagship for the invasion. It was one of the Union vessels that had slipped away from the Battle of Galveston during truce time.

The *Clifton* and ships following it stayed far enough out from the coast so as not to be seen. Toward late evening, Crocker led the ships closer to shore in order to see the signal light of the *Granite City*, which was supposed to be waiting for them. Seeing no light, Crocker moved his vessels on further. Before long, he realized that he had almost reached Galveston. He turned the ships back but still could not find the light of the *Granite City*. Continuing the search until daylight, he finally found Lamson and his ship 30 miles east of the Sabine River in a little cove off the coast of Louisiana.

Lamson left his ship to meet with Crocker and Weitzel aboard the *Clifton*. Crocker demanded an explanation of why he was not at Sabine. Lamson related his story of going to Sabine Pass and not finding blockade ships waiting. He told Crocker that he waited for awhile then sighted a very large ship painted dark gray. He just knew it was the *290*. Fearing an attack from the dreaded ship, he left. Crocker and Weitzel, now realizing there was no way to pull a surprise attack, decided to wait until September 8 to enter the pass.

Back aboard the *Granite City*, Lamson left for Sabine Pass. Crocker, concerned about Lamson's dependability, sent the *Arizona* to trail behind him to keep watch until the pass was reached. When the two vessels reached the waters outside the pass, other ships already there scattered. Lamson started delivering the message that the battle would not start until Tuesday and that the *Clifton* would enter the pass first. If Crocker found a good place to drop anchor, he would signal the rest of the ships. However, Lamson fouled up again. He stopped the ships at the rear of the fleet and delivered the important message, but he failed to stop the ones in the lead.

On September 4 when Magruder learned a large Union force was on its way from New Orleans, he started sending messages to Texas ports. He did not know where the enemy would strike, but all ports should be ready. Commodore Leon Smith in Beaumont did not receive the message until three days later. He immediately sent telegrams to Magruder and other officers asking for help. A few soldiers in Orange boarded the little steamer, *Josiah H. Bell*, and headed for Sabine. Leon Smith rounded up 95 men in Beaumont and set out for the pass on another steamer, the *Roebuck*. The Davis Guards were still working to rebuild Fort Griffin. In addition to reinforcing walls, they had constructed bombproof shelters and several underground rooms to store arms and ammunition. Their only heavy guns were six old cannons, in poor shape for firing, which had been moved from a ship and from an abandoned fort.

Dowling and his men made sure the old cannons were in place and in working order. Borrowing a farmer's wagon, some of the Texans moved all their ammunition, which had been stored in an old house, to one of the protected underground areas inside the fort.

Cries of "The Union is coming" spread around the little town. The townspeople remembered the last autumn when they had watched from the top of a house while the Union destroyed their fort. They remembered seeing the Union men move north to Beaumont and later hearing they had burned the railway depot and a railroad over Taylor's Bayou. At that time, over half of the citizens were too ill with yellow fever to leave Sabine City. This time, they intended to stay even if there were no epidemic holding them. The Davis Guards needed them.

One farmer dug bushels of sweet potatoes and started cooking them. Another one killed a beef, butchered it, and sent it to various homemakers to cook. Women went to work making bread, biscuits, and other foods that would be needed at the fort. They planned to deliver hot coffee to the Guards throughout the coming battle.

Usually, the Guards stayed in town, but now they remained at the fort while Captain Odlum commanded the post from Sabine City. The captain tried but was unable to reach the 10 or 12 men on leave, one of whom was Dick Dowling's brother. However, the Guards were confident they could put up a good fight even without those who were gone.

On Monday, September 7, when flashing lights out in the Gulf were followed by two large ships coming to the mouth of the pass, the Davis Guards manned their guns. They held their positions, alert to all enemy moves. Later in the morning, nine vessels came into the entrance of the pass. Dowling and his men were puzzled when they suddenly turned and went back out into the Gulf. Odlum immediately sent a report to Magruder.

In a short time, Odlum received orders from Magruder to blow up the fort and retreat at least 10 miles toward Beaumont. Magruder added that it would be useless to fight against several thousand Union troops with fewer than 50 men and only six old, unstable guns. Odlum rushed the orders out to Dowling. As Dowling read the orders, he noticed a note that Odlum had scribbled on them, "Use your own discretion about giving battle."

Dowling called his troops together and read the orders aloud. He watched the men's faces closely when they discussed the situation. How many wanted to leave? How many wanted to stay? All the Fighting Irishmen were in favor of fighting.

13

Battle of Sabine Pass

With Lamson's bungling and other errors made, Crocker felt that any attempt at making a surprise attack was gone. He proposed, "Why don't we run for the Sabine at once and attack with what we have? I went in there with just a handful of men last October." Several other officers disagreed with such a move. After more discussion, they decided to send the *Clifton* into the pass early on the eighth, fire a few shells then signal other warships to enter the pass if it were safe to navigate.

Early on September 8, 1863, the Texans could see lights flashing signals to the ships. The *Clifton* entered the pass and started firing at 6:30 A.M. In one hour, 26 shells came at Fort Griffin, but only two hit, doing very little damage. The Davis Guards, alert at their guns, held their fire.

About 9:00 A.M. two ships steamed straight into the pass. Troops were landed on a sandbar in the channel within shooting range of the fort. After the soldiers landed, the *Sachem*, followed by the *Arizona*, moved still farther into the channel. Nearing the fort, the *Sachem* began firing. Still no answer came from the fort. In the meantime, the *Clifton* came in behind the *Arizona* with guns blazing. By then, the *Sachem* had moved up the channel to the poles that the Guards had practiced shooting at for weeks.

The Davis Guards at Sabine Pass

Instantly, Dick Dowling fired the first shot then gave his men the signal to shoot. A roaring noise and black smoke filled the air over the fort. Splinters of wood scattered all around. The *Arizona*, moving in behind the *Sachem*, started firing, but Dowling ignored it. He was keeping an eye on the *Sachem*. It had to be stopped. Once past this critical point, it could move into the unprotected rear of the fort for attack.

One shell from the Davis Guards' 24-pound cannon hit its mark, tearing completely through the hull of the *Sachem*. With all the fort's guns firing, there was hit after hit. Many Union men fell as their vessel's deck was torn to shreds. Unable to turn, the crippled *Sachem* steamed on. Suddenly, it was caught in a fast, swirling current and swept into a mud bank. While the Union gunners continued to fire, they sent a signal to other ships to come tow them off the mud bank. As the *Arizona* moved closer to the *Sachem*, a Davis Guard's shell took away one of its masts. Another shot hit its boiler. Steam and boiling hot water sprayed into the air and gushed over the deck. Union troops had to jump over the sides of the ship to escape being burned.

In the meantime, Crocker's *Clifton* moved closer, firing rapidly, creating huge holes in the fort's earthen walls. Just as Dowling stepped back from sighting his 32-pounder, his gun was hit, but he was not hurt. Almost immediately, another of the fort's guns was struck, throwing metal fragments into the air. By now, the Guards were firing so fast that there was no time to swab the guns to cool them. The cannons were so hot that some of the gunners were suffering burned hands.

Only 300 yards from the fort, the *Clifton* was hit. With wheel ropes for steering destroyed, the helpless vessel swerved into a muddy bank and stopped. Then, more of the Guards' shells hit the boiler causing it to explode. For the second time, Union troops had to jump from their ship to get away from scalding steam and gallons of boiling water.

Throughout the day, Sabine City people traveled back and forth to the fort. Odlum and his men went to see if anything were needed. The town doctor rode out to help should someone be wounded. Housewives traveled back and forth in buggies and wagons carrying fresh food and hot coffee to the Davis Guards.

Lamson, aboard the *Granite City*, was watching all this movement through a spyglass. He saw many people entering the rear of the fort amid heavy dust. He could see soldiers jumping from the disabled ships. Panic-stricken, he assumed all the confusion was being caused by reinforcement troops entering the back of the fort. So he signaled other Union vessels that Texan artillery had come to help Dowling and his men. He just knew the Texans would destroy the crippled ships.

After receiving Lamson's message, General William Franklin, who had directed landing of the troops, ordered the rest of the fleet to retreat. Seeing the *Sachem* and *Clifton* raising flags of surrender, Lamson turned and headed full steam for the Gulf of Mexico. While Lamson and the fleet were leaving, three little Confederate gunboats, the *Josiah H. Bell*, the *Roebuck*, and the *Florilda* arrived on Sabine Lake. Help had finally come from Beaumont and Orange, but it was too late. The battle was over.

Twenty-five-year-old Dowling, carrying a white, powder-stained flag of truce on his saber, boarded the grounded *Clifton*. Wearing no shirt and blackened from head to foot with gunpowder, he faced Crocker. The Union leader took one look at him and almost refused to believe that this red-headed boy and a handful of Texans had defeated the Union fleet. Two gunboats, 14 guns, much ammunition, and 472 prisoners were captured by the Davis Guards. Also, of course, several gunboats and about 5,000 to 6,000 troops were chased away. Not one Fighting Irishman was killed or wounded.

President Jefferson Davis sent words of praise to the Texans who fought and held the fort at Sabine. Special honors went to Dick Dowling and his men for preventing invasion and occupation of Texas. General Magruder held a ceremony in which he gave sabers to the officers of the

Dick Dowling

Davis Guards and special caps with "Sabine" written across them to the soldiers.

President Davis later called the battle at Sabine Pass "the greatest military victory in the world." The only medals issued by the Confederacy during the Civil War went to the Fighting Irishmen. Made from Mexican silver dollars, they had "Battle of Sabine Pass, September 8, 1863" engraved on one side. On the back of the coins were two letters, "DG," for Davis Guards. Also, Sabine City was renamed Sabine Pass in honor of the battle fought there.

14

The Rio Grande Campaign

After being defeated at Galveston and Sabine Pass, the Union already had enough worries trying to blockade Texas. Then, in 1863, another serious problem arose. It started with Mexico's failure to pay debts owed to several European countries. Three different political groups divided Mexico's government. It had been in a turmoil for many years and finally became bankrupt in 1859. Leaders of the various parties tried to borrow money from the United States and Europe. One of the political parties managed to secure loans of several million dollars from European countries. In the year 1861, shortly after the Civil War started, Benito Pablo Juárez, recognized as the president of Mexico by the United States, stopped payments on the foreign debts and took over property owned by European countries.

A few months later, in 1862, France, England, and Spain joined together in sending troops to occupy the Mexican port of Vera Cruz. They planned to stay until the Mexican government paid the money owed them. Later, when England and Spain learned that France was planning to invade Mexico, they made a settlement with Mexico and left, unwilling to risk being involved should France start a war. With the excuse that he was trying to collect debts, French ruler Napoleon III invaded Mexico

Benito Juárez

in 1863. The Union, fearing that France would make an alliance with the Confederates, hurried to blockade Texas ports past Galveston and Sabine Pass all the way to the Mexican border.

Just a few weeks after the battle at Sabine Pass, the Union moved part of its navy into the mouth of the Rio Grande. First, they took the island of Brazos de Santiago, at the entrance to the Rio Grande's mouth, then they moved on to occupy Port Isabel. Knowing that Brownsville would be next, the hopelessly outnumbered citizens set fire to their town on November 5 and left. Even with the port burned and all people gone, the Union moved into Brownsville with 7,000 men.

While the Rio Grande naval operation continued, Banks sent other Union forces along the Gulf to capture Corpus Christi, Aransas Pass, and Indianola. After Union successes there, only the ports of Galveston and Sabine Pass were still occupied by Texans. For the first time, Texas' trade suffered. In order to continue trading by way of Mexico, Texans had to move their trade route farther north. Not only was the northern route miles out of the way, but the area was in constant danger of attack from warlike Indians and Mexican bandits.

15

The Red River Campaign

By late 1863, the president was still concerned about French occupation of Mexico and the amount of cotton passing across the Rio Grande. Since summer, Lincoln had been hearing rumors that Texas was considering becoming a republic under the protection of Napoleon III. The rumors were said to have come from Frenchman Alphonse Dubois de Saligny, Napoleon's minister in Mexico. The French minister had lived in Texas twice. For awhile in the early 1840s, he was in

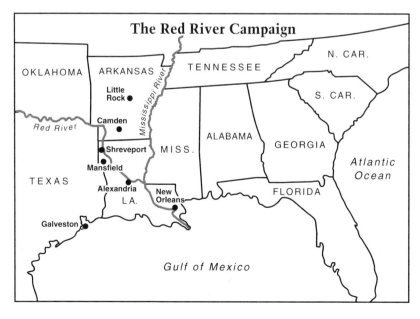

The Red River Campaign

Austin spying on the new republic. Later, the French legation in Washington sent him back to the capital. He built a home there that was also used as the French Embassy. During that time, he accumulated many debts that he refused to pay; then, he became involved in the "Pig War" when his landlord's pigs wrecked flowers around the embassy.

Huge shipments of cotton were still reaching Matamoros and Bagdad, even though the blockade had been extended all the way to the Mexican border. Lincoln's military leaders kept him informed about the problem. In a letter to E. R. S. Canby, the president talked about the amount of cotton passing through the Texas blockade and the enormous amount of money the Texans were earning, adding, "You know how this keeps up his armies at home, and procures supplies from abroad. . . . It becomes immensely important to us to get the cotton away from him."

Late in 1863, after meeting with several of his leading officers, Lincoln sent orders to General Banks to invade the Lone Star State by way of the Red River. This river not only furnished a good entry route from New Orleans, but it also ran through an area where thousands of bales of cotton were stored. The Union would seize this valuable product as it swept toward Texas.

When Kirby Smith was informed of Banks' planned invasion, he put out a call for troops. Magruder sent all available Texans. Among them were Tom Green, William Scurry, and Charles Pyron, who fought together in Sibley's army. Tom Green left for Louisiana with several cavalry regiments under his command. Members of these units were expert riders and sharpshooters. All were experienced in battle tactics. Two of them were foreign-born. One was Debray Xavier, who was born in France and graduated from the French Military Academy. Another was German August Buchel, who fought in Turkey and Spain (where he was knighted by the queen), before moving to Texas.

Pyron left from Galveston with his infantry, which drew much attention as it traveled to Louisiana. The regiment—about 400 soldiers dressed in many different types of clothing—marched with a huge Confederate flag waving in the air and a band of eight or ten instruments playing. All the men were armed with guns and Bowie knives, ready to join Taylor's army. Major General Richard Taylor, son of former U.S. President Zachary Taylor and brother-in-law of Jefferson Davis, was commander of the forces assembled in Louisiana.

General Banks, who had suffered defeat in each battle with Texans except in the Rio Grande campaign, left for Shreveport early in March, 1864. The start of the campaign had been delayed until winter when early spring rains would cause the river to rise enough for ships to pass over a shallow falls area near Alexandria. But, so far that year, there had been little rain. Banks led an army of 30,000 troops along an inland Louisiana road while Rear Admiral David Porter commanded a flotilla of 60 vessels, 22 of which were armed, up the Red River.

While Banks and Porter were moving toward Shreveport, Union General Frederick Steele left Little Rock, Arkansas, which he had captured early in the fall of 1863. He was headed toward Shreveport to combine his 15,000 troops with those of Banks but never managed to reach there. He was stopped in Camden, Arkansas, by Confederate Major General Price, who defeated him thoroughly with only half as many men. Price, forced out of Little Rock by Steele several months before, was elated by the victory.

As Porter's ships steamed up the river, his men stopped along the way in village after village to seize tons of cotton. Texas scouts had several fights with

Union men as they rode along the river, trying to burn all stores of cotton before Porter's flotilla captured them.

When Taylor received word that Banks' army would be passing through Mansfield, a small town 40 miles south of Shreveport, he moved his troops there, set up a plan for battle, and waited. On April 8, as Banks' advance unit of men neared Mansfield, they were attacked by over 8,000 of Taylor's soldiers. The Texans defeated them and captured 150 wagons loaded with supplies, 22 cannons, and 2,500 prisoners.

After the battle, under cover of darkness, Banks' army slipped away to Pleasant Hill, 20 miles south of Mansfield. The next day, more men arrived to help Taylor. With 11,000 soldiers, the Texans marched to Pleasant Hill. When they attacked the Union troops, part of Banks' men held the Texans back while another part of them retreated. The Union soldiers were in such a hurry that they left some of their ships. Porter's flotilla rushed on toward Alexandria but was stopped by a drop in the river's water level. The falls area became so shallow that the ships could not pass.

Aware that the ships were stuck, the Texans separated into groups of about 2,000 men and traveled south, planning to stop the retreat by blockading the river below Alexandria. Before they reached there, though, the ships were saved by a Wisconsin engineer. Union Colonel Joseph Bailey was a former lumberman, who engineered the cutting of trees and the building of a series of dams. His work caused enough water to back up to allow Porter's ships to pass on along the river.

From April 15 through May 5, one Texan unit at a time caught up with the flotilla of boats. They engaged in battle after battle along the Red River, damaging many of the ships. Casualties were heavy among the Texans who had to fight from the banks of the river with little or no protection. General Tom Green was killed at

Blair's Landing on April 12. Then, on April 30, General Scurry lost his life at Jenkins' Ferry. Both Texans were buried in the State Cemetery in Austin with military honors.

During the fights below Alexandria, Porter lost more ships. The *Eastport* and *Champion No. 5* were sunk first, then the *Champion No. 3* was captured by Texans. A short time later, Taylor's men also took the *Warner* and the *Signal*. The only ships the Union managed to keep were badly damaged. Banks had failed completely, defeated again by Texans before he even reached Texas. When he returned to New Orleans, he was relieved of field command but was still kept on duty in southern Louisiana.

16

Surrender

Confederate optimism about the war crumbled as 1865 came. The South was facing defeat, not from a lack of military skill or efficient troops, but from a shortage of arms, food, and clothing.

On Sunday afternoon, April 9, Lee met with Grant in the village of Appomattox Courthouse. In the home of Wilmer McLean, Lee sat at a marble table, dressed in his finest uniform with his sword hanging at his side. The blade of the sword was inscribed "Help Yourself and God

This photo of Lee was taken one week after Appomattox.

will help you." Grant sat at a small pine table in a shabby, mud-spattered suit. The Union general, wishing for peace, offered mild terms of surrender. Feeling the terms were fair, Lee surrendered. The usual practice of a defeated officer's turning over his sword to the victor did not take place. Lee did not offer it, and Grant did not ask for it. According to the terms, Confederates were paroled instead of being arrested as prisoners of war and were allowed to keep their horses and sidearms. Each man was allowed to return home.

When Lee left the McLean house, Grant and his men removed their hats and stood at attention. Lee mounted his faithful horse, Traveller, and rode to meet his waiting 28,000 troops. He thanked his soldiers for their unsurpassed valor and courage. The half-starved, ragged troops, some of whom were barefoot, crowded around, touching him and Traveller to show their admiration and loyalty. Lee shook hands with many of them and wished them a safe return home as he rode away. Grant stood watching Lee until he was out of sight.

After Lee left, the McLean house furniture and other household objects were put up for sale at two $10 gold coins each. General Philip Sheridan bought the pine table and gave it to George Armstrong Custer as a gift for Custer's wife. The famous Indian fighter left the meeting astride his horse with the table balanced upside down on his head.

Other surrenders would come. News of Lee's action in Appomattox had not yet reached the armies of Johnston in North Carolina, Maury's forces at Mobile, Forrest's armies in Alabama, or Kirby Smith's in the Trans-Mississippi region.

A week before Lee surrendered, he sent a note to Davis that Richmond must be evacuated. Davis and his cabinet left that night and went to Danville,

United States Army General Ulysses S. Grant

carrying $500,000 worth of government gold. They were guarded by the famous sea raider, Admiral Semmes. When Davis learned of Lee's surrender, he and his men fled to Greensboro, then south across the Carolinas on a wagon train. Five small cavalry brigades accompanied them.

Less than a week after Davis and his men left Virginia amid the turmoil caused by Lee's surrender, President Lincoln was assassinated. While attending a play at Ford's Theater in Washington, he was shot by actor John Wilkes Booth and died on April 15. More confusion came as Vice President Andrew Johnson assumed the office of president and worked to restore order.

In the last meeting between Davis and his cabinet, a decision was reached to quit fighting, end the Confederate government, and return home. But, by then, Davis was being pursued by the Union as a fugitive and was not able to go home. On May 10, one month after he left Virginia, the Confederate president and his escorts were captured near Irwinville, Georgia. Harsh feelings against the Confederates were running high in the North. Many Northern leaders considered Southern leaders to be traitors and felt they should be convicted of treason and hanged.

Vice President Andrew Johnson became president when President Lincoln died.

Unaware that Davis had been captured three

days before, Kirby Smith called for a conference on May 13, 1865, to discuss continuing the war. Texas, Arkansas, Louisiana, and Missouri governors, together with several Southern generals, met at the home of Senator Wigfall in Marshall, Texas. (Louis T. Wigfall, a quick-tempered Confederate senator, had killed one man and wounded another in duels over political beliefs.)

The main issue discussed was the fate of the Confederacy. Should the Confederate army make a stand or should it quit fighting and surrender? The governors had already made up their minds and had drawn up surrender terms they would be willing to accept. Kirby Smith, however, did not agree with them. Several weeks before, he and Davis had discussed a plan in which Davis would meet him in Texas, make another stand against the Union, and keep fighting. The meeting ended without reaching an agreement.

Hoping Davis was on the way, Kirby Smith and a band of his troops hid horses in the heavily forested swamps of East Texas and waited. Time dragged on with no word from Davis, and one by one, Kirby Smith's men became discouraged and deserted.

Kirby Smith did not learn of Davis' capture until after he moved his headquarters to Houston on May 27. Efforts to continue the war now became hopeless. On June 2, he and Magruder boarded the steamer, *Fort Jackson*, anchored in the harbor at Galveston. The two Texans surrendered the Trans-Mississippi Department and gave up their swords to E. R. S. Canby, who had lost several battles to Sibley's Texans in New Mexico.

The last surrender of the war came the next day. Brigadier General Stand Watie, chief of the Cherokees, laid down arms on June 3, 1865.

17

Rip Ford and the Last Battle of the Civil War

The last battle of the Civil War took place a month after Lee's surrender. In 1864, Rip Ford was called again to assume duty along the Rio Grande, an area that he knew well. He and his Cavalry of the West left San Antonio and took over fort after fort along the Texas border. Ford still had received no money or supplies from headquarters but managed to seize horses, food, and arms as he and his men traveled.

By June 20, 1864, the Texas Rangers had captured almost 200 miles of Rio Grande borderland. Continuing toward Brownsville, Ford and his men came upon a unit of Union cavalrymen. They battled, and the Union was defeated, losing all wagons, horses, and equipment to the Rangers. Loaded with fresh supplies, Ford and his men moved southward to Brownsville. They were surprised to find no Union troops around when they moved into Fort Brown and raised the Confederate flag on July 30. They spent the next few months guarding the Rio Grande border.

In March, 1865, Union General Lew Wallace, who later became famous as the author of the historical novel *Ben Hur*, came to the Rio Grande to meet with Ford. He presented a plan, already approved by Lincoln, to drive the French out of Mexico. The Confederates, according to the plan, would surrender, join the Union, then work with the Mexican army to get rid of the French. Knowing the Confederates were in a weakened state, Ford thought Wallace's plan was worth considering, but his superior officer refused to discuss the matter. Wallace and Ford did accomplish one thing, though. They established a truce on the Rio Grande.

At this time, Colonel Theodore H. Barrett, a new Union officer, was in command at Brazos de Santiago. Added to his own regiment were a New York regiment of riflemen and some cavalry troops. Barrett had never seen combat duty. Eager to make a name for himself, he asked his commander for permission to provoke the Confederates. His commander refused and reminded him of the truce in effect. Against orders, Barrett prepared for a demonstration against Southern soldiers. He gathered troops on May 12, 1865, and marched to Palmito Hill, about 12 miles east of Brownsville. Arriving late in the afternoon, he and his troops were fired upon by some of Ford's Rangers. They immediately sent word to Ford that Union soldiers were in the area. Ford then sent messengers to headquarters to get permission to stop Barrett and his troops. When he received an answer ordering him to retreat, he was furious. Ford informed headquarters that the Confederate troops were under his command and that he intended to fight.

The next day, Ford and his cavalry reached Palmito Hill in the middle of a fight between the Union and Southern troops. Quickly, Ford arranged his men for battle then yelled: "Men, we have whipped the enemy in all previous fights. We can do it again. Charge!" Ford's 300

Texas Rangers plunged forward to defeat over 800 Union soldiers in the last battle of the Civil War. Not until after the battle did Ford hear from one of his prisoners that Lee had surrendered a month before.

Years later, while writing his memoirs, Ford confessed that when he saw the Union lines of two regiments and a company of cavalry at Palmito Hill, he thought to himself, "From the number of Union men I see before me, I am going to be whipped."

18

Texans and Confederates after Surrender

Even before the war was over, a few Confederates left the United States, but after Lee surrendered, thousands fled. Some went to Jamaica or Cuba, others to Canada, Brazil, or Europe; but most of them crossed the border to Mexico. Feeling they had done nothing wrong, many Southerners refused to face the humiliation and punishment they knew Northerners would heap upon them.

Texans and Confederate leaders fleeing to Mexico knew that changes in the Mexican government had taken place over the last couple of years. However, they were not aware of the dangerous unrest among the Mexican people brought on by the changes. One year after Napoleon III took over Mexico in the summer of 1863, he sent Austrian Archduke Maximilian to rule as emperor. Napoleon told the new ruler that the Mexican people wanted him, but Maximilian soon learned that he was not welcome. Most natives of Mexico considered Benito Juárez, an Indian lawyer, their leader.

When the new emperor arrived, Juárez left Mexico City and took his army north to begin assaults on the foreign leader. He made raids on Maximilian's soldiers,

Austrian Archduke Maximilian was sent by Napoleon III to rule as emperor of Mexico.

stole supplies, and destroyed communication systems. Outsiders furnished money to help Juárez drive the French from Mexico. One American, Union General Lew Wallace, collected donations from people of the North to help the Mexican lawyer. Juárez took the money from Wallace even though he did not like receiving help from him. He wondered if Americans helped him rid his country of the French, then who would help him get rid of the Americans?

After settling in Mexico, Maximilian traveled over many parts of his new country to observe the people and their living conditions. Sometimes he wore the type clothes worn by the natives, hoping to win approval from them. He made notes of needed improvements such as methods for growing food and other crops.

Maximilian had already given land grants to French, Austrian, and German immigrants. With Confederates pouring across the border, he wanted to find a place for them, too. Because they were already familiar with good planting methods, they could teach the Mexicans better ways to grow crops.

In September, 1865, the emperor set aside space for Confederate colonies in the area of Vera Cruz. He knew they would appreciate this land with its lush growing qualities. Its tropical, fertile soil was covered with palm, bamboo, and banana trees. The air was hot and damp with constant rainfall. Several provinces were settled by the Confederates. The one named Carlota was just a few miles off the imperial highway from Vera Cruz to Mexico City. General Sterling Price, former governor of Missouri who fought with Ben McCulloch during the war, drew up a list of regulations for law and order in the new colonies. For his work with immigration and land sales, he was awarded 640 acres at Carlota. Part of this land was set aside for a townsite, and the rest was used for his home and planting. After building his own house of adobe and bamboo, he planted large crops and cultivated them by hand.

Commodore Matthew Maury, a well-known oceanographer and naval astronomer, also helped with the colonies. He had come to Mexico after General Lee advised him to leave the United States for awhile. Maury had carried on experiments to develop a missile to destroy Union ships and was the first to find an effective use for torpedoes. At that time they were very crude, made of glass or stoneware bottles filled with gunpowder. He developed a method for attaching these explosives on the front of small ships to smash Union vessels below their metal protectors. The Confederate navy historian reported that this method damaged and destroyed more Union ships than any other weapon. Maury became one of the emperor's favorite advisers and was given a section of land at Carlota.

Along with other Texas leaders, Kirby Smith and Magruder also fled to Mexico. Kirby Smith, in the company of several other Texans, crossed the Rio Grande riding on a donkey. He traveled over 800 miles of sandy, arid plains filled with thorny cacti to Monterrey then boarded a horse-drawn vehicle to Mexico City. It took a month to travel the more than 1,200 miles from the border. Unable to feel settled in Mexico, he left and went to

Cuba. While there, he received a letter in April, 1866, informing him that he had been indicted for treason by the U.S. attorney general. Remaining in Cuba, he was later given permission by General Grant to return to the United States on probation. After reaching home, he served as chancellor at the University of Nashville then as president of the University of the South at Sewanee, Tennessee. Before his death in 1893, he was pardoned by the United States government.

One Texan who felt at home in Mexico was General Magruder, who had spent much time there during the Mexican War. After settling in Mexico City, he soon became a friend of Maximilian and helped him with immigration problems. The emperor was so impressed by Magruder's stylish clothes that he started dressing in the same way. Magruder had bushy sideburns and often wore salt and pepper colored cutaway suits, tall gray hats, and patent leather boots. He enjoyed giving lavish parties and attending social events. Later, when Maximilian lost power, Magruder returned to Texas and traveled around the state giving lectures on the war. When he died in 1871, he was buried in Galveston, the site of his most daring victory.

Instead of planting crops, some Confederates set up other businesses. Texan W. D. Johnson opened a hotel that also served as a center for social activities. Former Texas Senator and Chief Justice William Oldham opened a photography shop. General Joseph Shelby, who had served under General Price in Missouri, opened a freight company.

Stationed in Corsicana, Texas, at the time Lee surrendered, Shelby crossed the Mexican border with several hundred troops. After conducting a ceremony burying his Confederate flag in the Rio Grande, he led his army to Mexico City to meet with Maximilian. Right away, he and his men were told that they could settle in Mexico as individuals but not as a military group. Price made

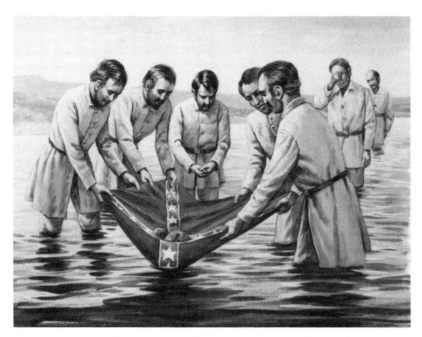

General Joseph Shelby buried the Confederate flag in the Rio Grande.

arrangements to live in a beautiful hacienda near Cordova. It had once belonged to Santa Anna, now in exile. After spending three unhappy years there, he and his family returned to Missouri where he died in 1873.

Two former Texas governors, Pendleton Murrah and Edward Clark, also fled to Mexico. Murrah died in Monterrey a short time after reaching there, but Clark stayed for awhile. He was another who was unable to adjust to life in Mexico and returned home to practice law.

While Texans and other Confederates were busy developing colonies, Maximilian learned that Napoleon was withdrawing his troops from Mexico. He felt forced to abdicate his office until his wife, Carlota, offered to go to France to talk with the French leader. She met with Napoleon, but he refused to honor the pact made with her husband to keep French military support in Mexico. While Carlota was still in France appealing to Napoleon, Juárez and his army advanced on Mexico City and forced Maximilian to leave the capital. Then, in March of 1867, the Mexican army seized the emperor. They executed him June 19, 1867, on a hill just outside Queretaro.

The hero at Sabine Pass, Dick Dowling, went back to Houston and opened a coffee and amusement club called "The Bank." Later, he became interested in the new oil industry. He traveled from place to place over the Lone Star State buying oil leases and was one of the first to drill an oil well in Texas. When an epidemic of yellow fever struck Houston, he died of the same sickness that had taken his parents' lives. Years later, in 1936, a large monument was erected at Sabine Pass honoring Dowling for what Jefferson Davis called "the most decisive battle of the Civil War."

Two famous Texas Rangers, Rip Ford and Henry McCulloch, also went home after the war. Ford became editor of the Brownsville newspaper, the *Sentinel*. Broad in both knowledge and experience, he served Texas in many ways. In 1872, he was delegate to the Democratic convention in Baltimore; in 1873, border cattle inspector; and then mayor of Brownsville in 1874. He helped with the Constitutional Convention of 1875 and served in the Texas Senate from 1876 to 1879. Later, he became superintendent of the State School for the Deaf and Dumb, where he worked to advance free education for all Texans. His last years were spent writing his memoirs and promoting interest in Texas history. As a charter member of the Texas State Historical Association, he wrote one of the first articles published in its quarterly journal. He died November 3, 1897, in San Antonio.

Henry McCulloch—Ranger, military leader, and statesman—gave his last years to supervising the State School for the Deaf and Dumb. He died on March 12,

1895, and was buried in the San Geronimo Cemetery in Seguin, Texas.

The daring leader of Hood's Brigade, John Hood, moved to New Orleans and married Anna Marie Hennen. On August 30, 1879, he died of yellow fever. A monument in memory of the brigade was erected on the grounds of the capitol in Austin. During World War II, an army camp was named in his honor.

Famous Texas Ranger, Indian fighter, and scout, Walter P. Lane, went back to Marshall and set up a business. When he died January 23, 1892, he was buried with military honors in Marshall. There a monument was erected in memory of his service to Texas.

After the war, Lawrence Sullivan Ross returned to his home in Waco, entered politics as a senator, then became governor. He was the first governor to occupy the new capitol building recently built in Austin. When he retired, he was elected president of A&M College. After he died on January 3, 1898, he was buried in Waco, and a statue was erected in his honor on the campus at College Station, Texas. Sul Ross University at Alpine was also named in his honor.

Another Texas military leader, General Sibley, fled to Africa. He joined the Egyptian army as a general of artillery from 1867 to 1874. In ill health, he finally returned to Virginia where he died August 23, 1886.

Captain Semmes, who helped Texas with the spectacular *290*, was rescued after his famous ship was sunk off the coast of France. He returned home to Mobile, was charged with both treason and piracy, and was jailed in a Washington prison. While serving time there, he was cleared of charges and elected probate judge in Alabama. Immediately, the U.S. secretary of war had him removed from office, declaring he was not eligible to hold an office even though he was recognized as the greatest naval hero of the Confederacy. Citizens in Mobile gave Semmes a beautiful home shaded by magnolia trees where he spent the rest of his life. He became a teacher at the state seminary in Alexandria, Louisiana, which grew into Louisiana State University.

Twenty-six families who migrated 5,000 miles to Brazil established permanent colonies. One Texan in the group was Calvin McKnight, a wealthy rancher and merchant. He and his friends worked hard to clear fast growing jungle foliage from their huge 200-acre farms. In addition to growing food, they planted cotton, sugarcane, and rice. They grew peach and pecan trees and cultivated grapes. One colonist from Georgia succeeded at growing watermelons, which became one of the colony's first cash crops. Other than planters, there were members whose skills helped fulfill needs for living in the primitive country. These were doctors, dentists, engineers, and teachers. Through the years, the American colonies grew to cover a large part of Brazil. Generation after generation held Southern customs but did learn to speak Portuguese, the official language of Brazil.

Strangely, two of the highest Confederate officers, President Jefferson Davis and General Robert E. Lee, received different treatment after surrender. President Davis was arrested and taken to Fortress Monroe in Virginia. Bound in chains, he was placed in a small, damp cell beside a moat. A light was kept shining in his face as guards paced up and down beside him day and night. Held prisoner for two years, he was not allowed to stand trial or to answer accusations against him. Even though many Union leaders insisted that he be convicted of treason and hanged, General Richard Taylor managed to obtain his release from prison. Davis was never brought to trial and was never pardoned. After he was released, he went to Biloxi, Mississippi, and spent his last years studying and writing. In 1881, he published a book about the rise and fall of the Confederacy. On December 9, 1889, he died and was buried in New Orleans. Four years later, his body was moved to Richmond, Virginia, where he once held office as Confederate president. His birthday is still observed as a legal holiday in several states, and three monuments honoring him stand in Texas.

General Robert E. Lee was not arrested but was called to Washington for interrogation by a committee of Northern leaders. These leaders asked question after question about the general's activities during the war. Lee answered each question honestly and rationally. After two hours, he was dismissed and returned home.

Even though the proclamation of 1865 barred Robert E. Lee from ever holding a public office again, he was determined to do whatever he could to help rebuild the South. He signed an oath of allegiance to the United States and sent it to Washington, but it was lost. Not until after his death was citizenship of his home country regained. His last years were spent in Lexington, Virginia, as president of Washington College. While presiding there, he supervised repair of the university and grounds, which were in ruins after the war; raised standards of learning; and started schools of journalism and commerce. Idolized by Southern people, Lee drew students from all parts of the South to study under him. As president of the university, he often spoke to the students, stressing that the South's recovery hinged upon the minds of the young and that it was important for them to become well educated to help in the recovery. Often, he closed his lectures with, "Young gentlemen, remember that the eyes of the South are upon you." One of Lee's students, William L. Prather, later became president of the new University of Texas. Remembering the impact of Lee's words, Prather often closed his own addresses with, "Students of the University of Texas, the eyes of Texas are upon you." Later, one of Prather's students wrote a song much used at football games and Texas celebrations, "The Eyes of Texas."

19

Reconstruction in Texas

Reconstruction was the term given to the period from the end of the Civil War until the time when the South was again accepted as part of the United States. The period varied in different states. In Texas, it lasted from 1865 to 1874.

Toward the end of the war, Lincoln had prepared a mild plan of reconstruction under which each state was to be restored to its original place when 10 percent of Southern voters pledged allegiance to the United States and accepted its laws. After Lincoln's death, the new president, Andrew Johnson, also wanted the South to reenter the Union without punishment. He proclaimed a pardon for all of the South except Confederate leaders, who would be required to take a loyalty oath.

At the time Reconstruction started, Con-

Union General Gordon Granger

gress was in control of radical members of the Republican party who wanted to punish the South. The radicals did everything they could to discredit the new president. They even spread rumors that Johnson helped with the assassination of Lincoln and was a drunkard. When Johnson continued to fight against harsh treatment for the South, the radicals passed a law taking away voting power of anyone who fought with the Confederates and placed the South under military control.

On June 10, a few days after Kirby Smith and Magruder surrendered, Union General Gordon Granger was sent to take control of Texas as military commander. When he arrived in Galveston on June 19, 1865, he immediately issued the following orders:

1. All slaves are now free. (June 19, Emancipation Day, is still celebrated in Texas.)
2. All Texas laws passed since March 1, 1861, must be annulled.
3. Names of all Confederate soldiers must be registered with United States officials.
4. Texas is now under charge of a military government.

After issuing the proclamation, Granger stationed soldiers in all major towns. One detachment of Union cavalry that came to help was led by George Armstrong Custer.

Custer, a West Pointer from Ohio, was a colorful soldier. He had long blond hair, wore a red tie around his neck, and carried a knife in the top of each of his tall cavalry boots. He and his cavalry arrived in Hempstead, Texas, in April, 1865. In the fall, he moved his troops to Austin and made his home and headquarters in the almost empty State School for the Deaf and Dumb. From the few people living there, he learned sign language and later sometimes used it to communicate with Indians. In sympathy with Texans and their problems, he refused to

let his troops treat them as conquered people. Custer's wife, Libby, was enchanted with Austin. She wrote that the capital was a "pretty town of stuccoed houses that appeared summery in the midst of the live oaks' perennial green." Custer's Austin home still stands on the edge of the University of Texas campus.

While Granger was setting up military control, Andrew J. Hamilton, a former Texas congressman who fought with the Union, was appointed provisional governor of Texas. An honest and conservative man, he had no hatred of the South and wanted to reunite his home state with the Union in peace. He had moved from Alabama to Texas in 1846 to practice law in La Grange. Later, he became attorney general of Texas then went to Congress where he protested against secession and refused to become a part of the Confederacy.

After arriving in Galveston, Hamilton (also called "Colossal Jack") went straight to Austin to organize a new state government. With almost no law enforcement after Texas' government collapsed at the end of the war, the state was open to abuse from thieves and outlaws. One group of outlaws even robbed the state treasury. Citizens had to take it upon themselves to form home guards and vigilance committees to protect their homes and communities.

First, Hamilton appointed officers to take charge of city, county, and state offices as well as the judicial system. He placed a few troops in major towns to help keep order. Then, he sent almost 50,000 soldiers to guard the Mexican border to let the French know they could not slip into Texas without being stopped. During the next two years, soldiers were also stationed at the polls to keep order during elections.

Hamilton's next job was to reunite Texas with the United States. To be readmitted, each state was required to draw up a new constitution, reject the secession constitution of 1861, give up slavery, and cancel debts made during the war. In order to write a constitution, voters were needed to elect delegates to a state convention. Since Texans no longer had the right to vote, they had to take an oath of allegiance to the United States and accept freedom of slaves before going to the polls.

In August, Hamilton chose chief justices in each county to administer the oath. November came before enough voters were registered to hold an election. It was January, 1866, before the election was held.

When the convention started on February 7, 1866, many disagreements arose among the delegates. There was so much bickering over ending secession and approving rights for slaves that little was accomplished. The delegates merely amended the former constitution by declaring secession was void and all Texas war debts no longer existed. Freed slaves would not be given equal rights but would be able to testify and be jury members when a black person was on trial.

When the convention adjourned in April, Hamilton called a general election. Since most Democrats could not vote, the Republicans, divided into radicals and conservatives, took over. Radical Elisha M. Pease and conservative James W. Throckmorton were nominated for the office of governor.

Pease, a lawyer, had served in various public offices and the legislature before becoming governor in 1853 and again in 1855. During his four years in office, much was accomplished. Railroad construction was encouraged; a new capitol was built; schools for the deaf, dumb, and insane were founded; and the state was almost freed of debt.

Throckmorton, who won the election, had also served Texas for many years. After leaving his practice as a doctor to fight in the Mexican War, he went into politics. As president of the secession convention, he was one of the eight who voted against leaving the Union. Unwilling to fight against Texas, he joined the Confederates. Placed in command of the Frontier District of Texas as Indian commissioner, he served in the Indian Territory, Arkansas, and Louisiana.

General Philip Sheridan

Throckmorton was inaugurated in August, 1866. Even though he worked to restore civil authority and courts, keep order, enforce laws, and improve frontier conditions, the new governor was constantly attacked by radical Republicans. Later, on July 7, 1867, military officials removed him from office as an "impediment to Reconstruction." The radicals welcomed "carpetbaggers." Carpetbaggers were people of the North who came south carrying all their possessions in a bag made of carpet material. They came seeking high-paying political jobs. Also, the radicals encouraged "scalawags," Texans who worked with the Union against the South. They even promoted the Ku Klux Klan, an organization that terrorized blacks to keep them away from polls during elections. When U.S. congressional elections were held in the fall of 1866, the radicals were victorious and soon replaced the existing program with a harsher one.

Under the new reconstruction plan passed by the United States Congress on March 2, 1867, these restrictions were placed on the South:

1. Southern governments were not recognized.
2. The South was divided into five military districts under the command of Union officers. (Texas and Louisiana were in the fifth district with General Philip Sheridan in command.)
3. Each state must ratify the U.S. Constitution's Fourteenth Amendment.
4. Each state constitution must give slaves the right to vote.

General Charles Griffin, already commander of the District of Texas, was given instructions to register voters for coming elections. In order to vote, each man had to pass the "ironclad" oath—swearing that he had never fought against the Union. This pledge, of course, barred thousands of Texans from voting.

Edmund J. Davis was elected governor of Texas in 1869.

The new reconstruction plan allowed Republicans to take complete control. In July, Texas radicals organized a state Republican party led by Elisha M. Pease. Despite his fight against stricter treatment of Texas, the radicals voted to draw up another constitution. When the constitutional convention met in Austin in June, 1868, only 12 members were Democrats; the rest were radicals, carpetbaggers, scalawags, and blacks. Edmund J. Davis was elected to serve as convention president.

Davis had studied law in Corpus Christi and practiced in the Rio Grande Valley. Later, he served as deputy collector of customs at Laredo then was elected district attorney at Brownsville. His district covered all of the lower Rio Grande Valley. During the war, he organized a cavalry regiment of Union men. His regiment spent part of the war in Louisiana then returned to Texas and caused trouble along the Rio Grande. When Davis and his cavalry started terrorizing people of the Rio Grande Valley in 1864, Rip Ford and his men drove them out of Texas. Davis would later suffer another defeat at the hands of Rip Ford.

While the convention was in session, Davis himself proposed dividing Texas into three states. For 92 days, the delegates fought over reasons to divide the state, ways to deal with frontier crime, and the issue of secession. After accomplishing nothing toward writing a new constitution, they recessed on August 31, 1868.

Convention delegates met again in December, 1868, and finally wrote a new constitution. Adopted by public vote early in 1869, it gave many new powers to the governor. Soon after its adoption, an election for a new governor was held. Davis, who had always wanted that office, was elected.

To complete reconstruction of Texas, the legislature passed the United States Constitution's Fourteenth Amendment freeing slaves. It also gave Davis control over voter registration, the state militia, and police force,

This building served as the capitol of Texas from 1853 until 1881. The Reconstruction Convention drafted the new state constitution here in 1868-69.

a control that caused much suffering among Texans. These were powers never held before by a Texas governor.

Finally, on March 30, 1870, after nine long years of strife, Texas was readmitted to the Union. Now that the state was in good standing with the United States, the ironclad oath was dropped, giving all Southerners the right to vote.

Restored voting power placed Texas Democrats in control of the next legislature. It had been a long time since they had a voice in the government of Texas. When the new congress assembled in Austin in January, 1873, it passed laws undoing many of the powers given to Davis. In a general election of state officers in December, Richard Coke, a Democrat, was elected governor of Texas. Coke had come to Texas to practice law in Waco. At the start of the war, he entered the Confederate army as a private then rose to the rank of captain before the war ended.

Richard Coke of Waco was elected governor in 1873.

Claiming the election was illegal, Davis refused to give up his office. He wired President Grant to send military aid, but the president refused. Then, Davis stationed armed guards outside the capitol to prevent Coke's entry and wired President Grant again; still Grant refused.

In the meantime, Coke talked with several trusted friends, among whom were Rip Ford and Henry McCulloch, about helping to keep peace when he took office. On January 12, 1874, Coke arrived to take over his duties as governor. He found Republicans still holding the capitol and armed guards still standing outside. Once again, Rip Ford, who had served Texas in crisis after crisis, came to the rescue.

Out of his office window, Davis saw Ford, now a tall, slender 60-year-old, riding straight toward the capitol. Behind him marched well-armed, angry Texas Rangers singing "The Yellow Rose of Texas." When Ford announced that he had come to support Coke for governor, Davis no doubt remembered the time the famous Ranger had chased him out of Texas.

When Coke tried to enter the capitol on January 19, 1874, the door was locked. Since he was now governor of Texas, and his new office was inside the capitol, his guards broke the door down, and he walked in. Outside, a military band played while a 102-gun salute was fired to celebrate the end of Reconstruction in Texas.

20

The Aftermath

At the end of the war, the Lone Star State was struggling through financial ruin, burdened with an $8 million debt. Among other handicaps, the state had to furnish men and weapons for both their home and Confederate military needs, suffer the reduced income from cotton trade, and overcome the loss of $40 million paid in taxes to the Confederacy.

Even though Texas did not have as much property damage as the Southern states east of the Mississippi River, some of its land and property was in shambles. Houston, once a neat, attractive town, was overrun with shacks and shabby shelters put up by refugees who poured into Texas toward the end of the war. Most large towns held crowds of ragged, poverty-stricken people who had no place to live and no way to earn a living.

Military hospitals still tried to take care of the many soldiers injured in battle or sickened by epidemics of yellow fever and smallpox, but they never had enough room for them. Long death lists of these men were often published in newspapers.

It was a long time before prisoner-of-war camps were cleared. More than 1,000 Union men were held in cow sheds along Houston railroads. At one time, as many as 600 soldiers existed in gullies near Camp Verde in Kerr

Returning soldiers often found the property in shambles.

County. A prison at Camp Groce near Hempstead consisted of four rows of crude, dirty shelters. Camp Ford, four miles northeast of Tyler, held the largest prison. Its 10 acres of land enclosed by tall 18-foot logs, sometimes held as many as 5,000 prisoners. The only shelter available was made when captives scooped out holes in a hillside.

Many Texans who had grown food and made a living on their farms came home to find their houses and land in ruins. Women and children had often been unable to take care of their farms and planting by themselves. With the men gone, there also had been little protection against outlaws and bandits who abused families, stole horses, and rustled cattle. Families had suffered from lack of necessities such as baking soda, salt, coffee, medicine, and paper. Vegetables such as sweet potatoes, corn, or okra were dried and used as a substitute for coffee. Medical supplies and medicines had been scarce. Quinine, an important medicine used to fight fevers, could not be found after foreign ships were stopped by the blockade. The only medicines available had been ones made from roots and herbs.

Schools suffered from shortages of teachers and textbooks. Even though male teachers were exempt from military duty, many left to fight in the war. Textbooks bought from the North were no longer available. It was 1862, the second year of the war, before a Southern publishing company was able to furnish readers, spellers, and grammars.

Slave troubles increased. Slaves were happy to be free but faced many problems. Many of them, unable to read or write, lacked skills needed for jobs other than planting, but they had no land or other resources to start their own farms. An unfounded rumor that each slave would receive 40 acres and a mule spread through the newly freed people even though state officers told them it was not true. They traveled from place to place searching for their land and mules but never found them.

The Ku Klux Klan worked to stop the slave vote. Members of this group, dressed in long flowing white

The Ku Klux Klan worked to stop the freed slaves from voting.

robes, paraded through slave areas after dark. As they walked, they moaned and cried in ghost-like voices that bad things would happen if freed slaves went to the polls. Sometimes, they dashed through areas on horses leaving blood-stained notes warning blacks not to vote.

Even though Reconstruction brought hardships to Texans, some good changes also came. The Freedman's Bureau, organized at the beginning of Reconstruction, made great strides in school systems. The bureau started thousands of schools where both young and old blacks learned to read and write. State government supported free public education, giving help not only to slaves but to the many white children who had never attended school. Welfare programs began providing care for the poor and insane. Public works programs built and repaired buildings, roads, and bridges. More equal taxation, fairer judicial systems, prison reforms, and rights for women were also gained.

After Texas was finally readmitted to the Union, it was years before Texans were able to return to a stable life and much, much longer before the bad feelings built up between the North and the South began to fade.

Bibliography

Anderson, Adrian N. *Texas and Texans.* Austin: Steck-Vaughn Company, 1972.

Ashcraft, Allan C. *Texas in the Civil War: a Resume History.* Austin: Texas Civil War Centennial Commission, 1962.

Barron, S. B. *The Lone Star Defenders.* New York and Washington: The Neale Publishing Company, 1908.

Bowman, John S., ed. *The Civil War Almanac.* New York: Bison Book Corporation (Facts on File, Inc.), 1982.

Boyer, Richard O. *The Legend of John Brown.* New York: Alfred A. Knopf, 1973.

Buenger, Walter L. *Texas History.* Boston, Mass.: American Press, 1983.

Catton, Bruce. *The Coming Fury.* Garden City, New York: Doubleday & Company, Inc., 1961.

Clark, Joseph L. *The Story of Texas.* Dallas: D. C. Heath and Company, 1955.

Commager, Henry Steele. *The Blue and The Gray.* New York: The Fairfax Press, 1982.

Connell, Evan S. *Son of the Morning Star.* San Francisco: North Point Press, 1984.

Conner, John E. *Your Texas and Mine.* Oklahoma City, Okla.: Harlow Publishing Corporation, 1960.

Connor, Seymour V. *Texas, the 28th State.* Austin and Dallas: Graphic Ideas, 1972.

Davis, Burke. *The Long Surrender.* New York: Random House, 1985.

Donald, David Herbert. *Liberty & Union.* Boston: Little, Brown, & Company, 1977.

Eaton, Clement. *A History of the Southern Confederacy.* New York: Macmillan Publishing Company, Inc., 1954.

Eibling, Harold H. *Foundations of Freedom.* Dallas: Laidlaw Brothers, 1973.

Fehrenbach, T. R. *Lone Star.* New York: American Legacy Press, 1983.

Flood, Charles Bracelen. *Lee, the Last Years.* Boston, Mass.: Houghton Mifflin Company, 1981.

Frantz, Joe B. *Texas.* New York: W. W. Norton & Company, 1984.

Garcia, Guillermo X. "Way Down South in Brazil's Dixie." Austin: *Austin American-Statesman*, July 3, 1989, p. A6.

Haley, James L. *Texas: An Album of History.* Garden City, New York: Doubleday & Co., Inc., 1985.

Hall, M. H. *Sibley's New Mexico Campaign.* Austin: University of Texas Press, 1960.

Hendrick, Burton J. *Statesmen of the Lost Cause.* New York: Literary Guild of America, Inc., 1939.

Henry, Robert Selph. *The Story of the Confederacy.* rev. ed., N.p.: Bobbs-Merrill Co., 1970.

Hofstadter, Richard. *The United States.* Englewood Cliffs, N.J.: Prentice-Hall, 1960.

Horgan, Paul. *Great River.* Austin: Texas Monthly Press, Inc., 1984.

Horner, Dave. *The Blockade Runners.* New York: Dodd, Mead, & Co., 1968.

Johnson, Ludwell H. *Red River Campaign.* Baltimore: The John Hopkins Press, 1958.

Kerby, Robert L. *Kirby Smith's Confederacy.* New York: Columbia University Press, 1972.

Nesmith, Frances. *The Story of Texas.* New York: Noble & Noble Publishers, 1963.

Nunn, W. C., ed. *Ten More Texans in Gray.* Hillsboro, Tex.: Hill Junior College Press, 1980.

Pearson, Procter, Conroy. *Texas: The Land and Its People.* Dallas: Hendrick-Long Publishing Co., 1987

Pierce, Gerald. *Texas Under Arms.* Austin: Encino Press, 1969.

Pratt, Fletcher. *Civil War in Pictures.* Garden City, N.Y.: Garden City Books, 1955.

Randall, J. G. *The Civil War & Reconstruction.* Lexington, Mass.: D. C. Heath & Company, 1969.

Reagan, John H. *Memoirs.* New York: The Neale Publishing Co., 1906.

Richardson, Rupert N. *Texas The Lone Star State.* Englewood Cliffs, N.J.: Prentice-Hall, Inc., 1970.

Rolle, Andrew F. *The Lost Cause.* Norman, Okla.: University of Oklahoma Press, 1965.

Simpson, Harold B. *Battles of Texas.* Waco, Tex.: Texian Press, 1967.

Steen, Ralph W. *Texas: Our Heritage.* Austin: Steck-Vaughn Company, 1962.

Tolbert, Frank X. *Dick Dowling at Sabine Pass.* New York: McGraw Hill, 1962.

Vandiver, Frank E. *Their Tattered Flags.* New York: Harper's Magazine Press in association with Harper & Row, 1970.

Wallace, Ernest. *Texas in Turmoil.* Austin: Steck-Vaughn Company, 1965.

Webb, Walter Prescott. *The Texas Rangers.* Austin: University of Texas Press, 1935.

Index

290 (ship). *See Alabama #290* (ship)

A

Aftermath of Civil War, 115–118
Alabama
  capital of Confederacy located in, 6
  secession of, 6
Alabama #290 (ship)
  construction and armament of, 62–63
  fear of, 65, 72, 73, 74
  Hatteras sunk by, 62
  illustration of, 63
  nicknamed the *290*, 62
  sinking of, 64
Albuquerque, New Mexico, 45
Alexandria, Louisiana, 88
American Anti-Slavery Society, 4
American Indians, 24–25
Anderson, Robert, 17
Antietam, Battle of, 36
Appomattox Courthouse, 90, 91
Aransas Pass, Texas, 84
Arizona (ship), 71, 73, 75, 78–79
Arizona Territory, 43
Arkansas, secession of, 21
Austin, Stephen F., 51
Austin, Texas
  Custer's home in, 107–108
  French Embassy at, 86
  Pig War at, 86

B

Bagdad, Mexico, 69
Bailey, Joseph, 88
Banks, Nathaniel
  commander of Rio Grande campaign, 84
  conduct of Red River campaign, 86, 87, 89
  plan for attack against Fort Griffin, 70, 71
Barrett, Theodore H., 95
Battles
  Antietam, 36
  Bull Run, Second Battle of, 36
  Chickamauga River, 34–35, 36
  chronology of major battles, 30–31
  east of Mississippi River, 29–38
  Galveston, 57–61

Gettysburg, 36
Glorieta Pass, 47
Hood's Texas Brigade and, 35–38
Knoxville, 35
last battle of Civil War, 94–96
Manassas, Second Battle of, 36
Murfreesboro, 34
naming of, 29
Perryville, 34
Pittsburg Landing, 34
Sabine Pass, 78–82
Sharpsburg, 36
Shiloh, 34
Sibley campaign in New Mexico, 41–49
Stone's River, 34
Terry's Texas Rangers and, 34–35
Baylor, John
  assistance with Sibley campaign, 41–43
  illustration of, 42
Bayou City (cotton-clad steamer), 57–60
Beaumont, Texas
  attack on, 51
  planned invasion of, 70
Bell, Henry H., 62
Benjamin, Judah Philip, 20, 21
Blockade of Southern ports
  ordered by President Lincoln, 17
  Texas coast ports, 50–56
Boats. *See* Ships
Booth, John Wilkes, 92
Brazil, as refuge for Confederate Texans, 104
Brazos de Santiago (island), 84, 95
Brown, John
  crusade against slavery, 4
  illustration of, 4
Brownsville, Texas. *See also* Fort Brown
  attacked by Juan Cortinas' bandits, 27
  burning of, 84
  cotton trade through, 69
  last battle of Civil War and, 94
  occupation by Union troops, 84
  Rip Ford as editor of the *Sentinel*, 102
Buchel, August, 86
Bull Run, Second Battle of, 36

C

California, 39–40
Camden, Arkansas, 87
Camp Colorado, 22, 35
Camp Ford, 116
Camp Groce, 116
Camp Verde, 115–116
Canby, E. R. S.
  capture of Confederate supplies by, 49
  defeat by Green's troops, 43–44
  maneuvers in New Mexico Territory, 46–47
  Smith's surrender to, 93
Cannons ("Twin Sisters"), 14, 44
Carlota (wife of Archduke Maximilian), 101–102
Carpetbaggers, 111
Carson, Kit, 45
Cavalry of the West, 94
Cave, Eber W., 10
Champion No. 3 (ship), 89
Champion No. 5 (ship), 89
Cherokee Indians, 24, 25
Chickamauga River, Battle of, 34–35, 36
Chickasaw Indians, 25
Choctaw Indians, 25
Civil War. *See also* Battles
  aftermath of, 115–118
  cost of, 1
  first confrontation in Texas, 14–16
  first shot fired at Fort Sumter, 17
  last battle of, 94–96
  reconstruction period afterward, 106–114
Clark, Edward, 10, 11–12, 101
Clifton (ship)
  and battle of Galveston, 60
  and battle of Sabine Pass, 71, 74–75, 78, 80, 81
Coke, Richard
  background of, 113
  difficulties in assuming governorship, 114
  elected governor, 113
  illustration of, 114
Confederate flag
  burial in Rio Grande (illustration), 101
  design of "Stars and Bars" flag, 21
  illustration of, 22

Confederate navy. *See also* Ships; Texas navy
  Alabama #290 (ship), 62–65
  Sumter (ship), 63–64
Confederate States of America. *See also* Secession
  cabinet members of, 20–21
  capital moved to Richmond, Virginia, 22
  Davis elected president of, 6
  districts of, 22
  flag of, 21
  illustration of, 3
  inability to produce military and other supplies, 18
  lack of transportation and manufacturing resources, 18
  Montgomery, Alabama as capital of, 6
  Stephens elected vice president of, 6
  surrender of Confederate army, 90–93
  Texas delegates to convention for formation of, 10
  trade with foreign countries, 17–18
  western district of, 24–28
Constitution of Texas. *See* Texas Constitution
Cook, Joseph J.
  background of, 52
  defense of Galveston, 52–53
Corpus Christi, Texas
  bombardment of, 51
  captured by Union troops, 84
Cortinas, Juan Nepomuceno, 27–28
Cortinas War, 27–28
Cotton
  growing without slaves, 9
  Red River campaign to halt trade of, 85–89
  stored at Houston, 70
  tended by slaves (illustration), 8
  Union attempts to stop trade through Mexico, 69–70
Cotton-clad steamers, 54, 57–60
Creek Indians, 25
Crocker, Frederick, 71, 74, 78, 81
Custer, George Armstrong, 91, 107–108
Custer, Libby, 91, 108
Custis, Mary, 16

Confederacy's trade with foreign
countries, 17–18
Texas trade hampered by occupation of South Texas ports, 84
Twiggs, David, 14–15, 17
"Twin Sisters" (cannons), 14, 44
Two Hundred-Ninety (290) (ship).
See Alabama #290 (ship)

U

Uncle Ben (gunboat), 67
Uncle Tom's Cabin (Stowe), 5
illustration of cover, 5
Union navy. *See also* Ships; Texas
ports
blockading of Sabine Pass, 67
early attacks on Texas ports, 51
loss of ships in Red River campaign, 89
number of ships and personnel,
50–51
plan for attack against Fort Griffin
and Sabine Pass, 70–72
ships in battle of Galveston,
58–60
ships in battle of Sabine Pass, 71–
75
sinking of the *290*, 64

V

Valverde, 44–45
Van Dorn, Earl
assistance from Ben McCulloch,
25–26
background of, 41
Sibley campaign and, 41
Velocity (ship), 67–69

Vera Cruz, Mexico
occupation by France, England,
and Spain, 83
refuge for Confederate Texans,
98–99
Virginia, secession of, 21
Virginia Point, 56

W

Wainwright, Jonathan M., 60
Walker, Leroy Pope, 20
Wallace, Lew
assistance to Benito Juárez, 98
Ben Hur, 95
establishment of truce on Rio
Grande, 95
Warner (ship), 89
Washington, Martha, 16
Watie, Stand
illustration of, 24
service to Confederacy, 24–25
surrender of, 93
Weitzel, Godfrey, 73–74
Weld, Theodore Dwight, 4
Western district of Confederacy,
defense of, 24–28
Western expansion of Confederacy.
See Sibley's campaign
Westfield (ship), 60
Wier, A. R., 59
Wigfall, Louis T., 35, 93

X

Xavier, Debray, 86

Y

"Yellow Rose of Texas" (song), 114